Rainbow Children

A Racial Justice and Diversity Program for Ages 5 to 8

Norma Poinsett
and
Vivian Burns

Judith A. Frediani, Developmental Editor

Unitarian Universalist Association

Production Editor: Brenda Wong
Editorial Assistant: Jacquelyn O'Sullivan
Text Designer: Suzanne Morgan
Cover Designer: Bruce Jones

ISBN 1-55896-292-1

10 9 8 7 6 5 4 3 2 1
99 98 97 96 95

Acknowledgments
Every effort has been made to trace the owner(s) of copyright material. We regret any omission and will, upon written notice, make the necessary correction(s) in subsequent printings.

"The Gift of Color" by Robin F. Gray. Copyright © 1995 by Robin F. Gray. Printed by permission of author.

The games listed in "Cooperative Games" are from *Everyone Wins! Cooperative Games and Activities* by Sambhava and Josette Luvmour, published by New Society Publishers, 4527 Springfield Ave., Philadelphia, PA 19143. Copyright © 1990 by Sambhava and Josette Luvmour. Reprinted by permission of the publisher.

The illustrations of a cornucopia in Handout 5 and a Kwanzaa table in Handout 8 are from *The Kwanzaa Coloring Book* by Valerie J. R. Banks, illustrated by Sylvia Woodward, published by Sala Enterprises. Copyright © 1987. Reprinted by permission of the publisher.

The illustration for Handout 7 "The Rainbow Team," is by Janet Lane.

Contents

Introduction

This is a program of affirmation. It affirms the inherent worth and beauty of self, family, community, and human diversity. It is also an antibias curriculum that focuses on racial and ethnic prejudice. We like to believe that our young children are free of racism and that we can somehow protect them from prejudice through our family and religious values and practices.

But as early childhood specialist Louise Derman-Sparks points out in the *Anti-Bias Curriculum: Tools for Empowering Young Children*, "Although there is a great deal more to know about how children 'go about forming the intricate maze of knowledge and values' that result in self-identity and attitudes, we know enough not to underestimate the power of children to perceive the negative messages in their world or the power of those messages to harm them. It is too dangerous for early childhood educators to take an 'ostrich-in-the-sand' stance."

Children as young as two years are aware of differences in color, gender, and physical ability, and are also aware that those differences are connected with privilege and power. Consider one example that Derman-Sparks offers from a preschool:

> A 2 1/2-year-old Asian child refuses to hold the hand of a Black classmate. "It's dirty," he insists. At home, after bathing, he tells his mother, "Now my hair is white because it is clean."

What messages has this child received? What messages are our children receiving?

Eliot Eisner, in *The Educational Imagination: On the Design and Education of School Programs*, explains that all schools teach the same three curricula: the explicit, the implicit, and the null. Maria Harris, in *Fashion Me a People: Curriculum in the Church*, extends this analysis to religious education.

The explicit curriculum is what we *say* we are teaching; it is written in our prospectus, in our teacher guides, in our letters to parents. The implicit curriculum includes what we do or say in the context surrounding the explicit curriculum, actions which may support or undermine the explicit curriculum. For example, our explicit curriculum may say that we value racial and ethnic diversity, but if all the pictures on the walls of our churches are of and by white people, and African-American worship leaders appear only on Martin Luther King Day, our implicit curriculum is contradicting our stated goals and values.

While both the explicit and implicit curricula are actions we take, the null curriculum is a paradox because it is what we do *not* do or say or even think of. It includes the issues we don't talk about, the methods we don't try, the people we don't listen to, the fears we don't express.

For children in our congregations, racism can be a null curriculum because we don't feel comfortable addressing it and because we falsely believe that our silence somehow protects our children from racism's harmful effects. In reality, silence is not "golden" or even neutral. It conveys a message about what we truly value. If we do not clearly communicate our prodiversity, antibias values to our children and to ourselves, other messages will prevail.

As Carol Brunson Phillips points out, "It has been said that actions more often than not speak louder than words. And if this is so in the case of child-rearing, then we must be especially vigilant in our actions to shape the values children will attach as they learn about the people in their world. If we don't, they will *learn by default* the messages that are already prevalent out there and both we and they will contribute to perpetuating past ideas which we do not want to replicate in our children's future." (*Emphasis added.*)

The Reverend Mark Morrison-Reed has said that nobody is born a racist, but that racism is a role we are taught and then asked to play. This curriculum is an invitation from the Racial Justice Curriculum Team of the Unitarian Universalist Association to teach our children (and ourselves) that racism is not a role we want to play. It gives us an opportunity to express our religious values, particularly our belief in the inherent worth and dignity of all people and the interconnectedness of the human family.

Because we do our children an injustice if we deny reality, *Rainbow Children* acknowledges the reality of racial injustice and prejudice at conceptual levels this age group can understand. And because the best antidote for hatred is self-esteem, *Rainbow Children* is about *our own* worth and dignity, for when we are sure of the goodness within us, we have no need to hurt others.

Goals

The goals for participants are:

- To feel comfortable with themselves and this group
- To share their knowledge and feelings about self, family, and community
- To affirm the uniqueness of self and every other individual, and to value human diversity
- To see oneself and all people as members of one "rainbow race" with the same human rights and needs
- To gain an understanding of, at developmentally appropriate levels, the concepts of prejudice, racism, and racial justice
- To know that racial prejudice exists and is morally wrong
- To gain an understanding of society as multiracial and multicultural, and to feel positively about people of racial, ethnic, and cultural backgrounds different from their own

- To gain an understanding that families come in many shapes and sizes, and to affirm their own and others' families
- To feel good about themselves as loving, creative, and competent people.

This program expresses the Unitarian Universalist principles adopted by the UUA in 1985, especially these:

- The inherent worth and dignity of every person
- Justice, equity, and compassion in human relations
- The right of conscience and the use of the democratic process
- The goal of world community with peace, liberty, and justice for all.

The Program

Rainbow Children is a 12-session curriculum for children ages five to eight. The program includes 14 sessions because it provides options for the last two sessions. If used in the fall term, *Rainbow Children* culminates in a Kwanzaa celebration; in the spring term, it concludes with a celebration of *Cinco de Mayo*. Each session is scripted to last 55 to 60 minutes. Implementing this program requires other resources in addition to this leaders' guide. (See the list of required resources that follows this introduction.)

Leaders

Co-leaders are always an asset to the classroom, but they are a necessity in *Rainbow Children*. It would be difficult, if not impossible, for one person to guide a group of young children through the crafts and other activities in this program. If you do not have two or more teachers who can make a commitment to 12 sessions, be sure to recruit dependable helpers to support the leader.

Leaders should not only be good with children of this age group, they should be committed to prodiversity, antibias philosophy and action. This does not mean that leaders should be without prejudice—none of us are. But leaders should be aware of their attitudes, beliefs, and feelings around the issues of this program and be open to learning along with the children. A racially diverse teaching team is ideal, but if this is not possible, consider ways to enrich the program with guests, helpers, or field trips that expand the children's experiences with people of diverse backgrounds.

Environment

The meeting space is very important. Ideally, it should be bright and large, with ample wall space for displaying resources and the children's creations. It should have enough carpeted floor space for the group to sit in a circle, as well as worktables, chairs, and a small worship table.

The classroom environment provides an important opportunity to reinforce the values and goals of this program. It is not enough to *say* that the world is multicultural and that we value diversity. Let the environment speak, too, with multiracial and multicultural posters, calendars, pictures, banners, and/or other artwork on the walls. Be sure that books, crayons, dolls, puzzles, and other toys in the room are inclusive of race, ethnicity, culture, gender, and physical ability.

Program Structure

Each session includes goals, which state the participants' learning objectives; background information for leaders, which places the session in a larger context; a materials list; preparation instructions; and a session plan.

When something must be done a week or more before the session, this is indicated in the previous session. Preparation is just one reason that it is important to read the entire program before beginning, and to read ahead periodically to be prepared.

The sessions generally include the following:

Opening: Each session begins with a simple ritual that includes sitting in a circle, lighting a candle or chalice, and sharing a thought. The flame should be extinguished at the end of the closing. Children of this age enjoy the continuity of ritual and benefit from the sense of commu-

nity it creates. If the children come to the program directly from a worship time together, the opening ritual can be omitted and the group can simply sit in a circle and begin the focusing section.

Focusing: This section introduces the theme of the session, gives the children an opportunity to express what they already know or feel about it, and engages them in the topic through an activity.

Exploring: This section provides new information or perspectives on the theme, often through a story that invites the children to explore and interact with the new ideas.

Integrating: To help them integrate or internalize the new learnings, participants engage in a creative activity that helps express and make meaningful what they have learned.

Closing: Although the elements of the closing may vary—song, movement, verbal sharing, fruit communion—it provides a ritual of coming together in a circle of community to represent the special time that has been shared. If you do not have the time or the need for both an opening and closing ritual, choose one that works best for your group and offer it consistently.

Reflection and Planning

Leaders are usually very busy people who are eager to leave after class, but if co-leaders agree to spend even 5-10 minutes immediately after each session to reflect on how the program is going and what needs to be done for next time, both the leaders and the children will benefit. When leaders share their experiences regularly, they often feel less isolated and frustrated and more confident and organized. Co-leaders may agree at the start of the program whether they would welcome candid feedback from the other regarding their leadership style.

Parents

Parents and other adults in the home are an important part of a child's religious education. To enrich the children's experience with this program and to avoid misunderstandings about its themes, invite parents and interested others to a presentation and discussion of *Rainbow Children* before you begin. Share with them your philosophy and goals in offering this curriculum. Describe or engage them in some of the activities. Invite them to share their hopes and concerns, and encourage them to contribute their diversity to the program as helpers, storytellers, cooks, artists, or other resource persons.

Field Trips

Although no field trip is scheduled in this curriculum, you might consider one. The larger community offers a variety of multiracial and multicultural experiences for children, such as concerts, museum or library exhibits, multicultural fairs, restaurants and neighborhoods, social service projects with multicultural leadership, and so on.

If you decide to enrich the program in this way, look for people in your congregation who have knowledge or experience with the focus of the field trip. Also, consider inviting the children's families or the entire church family to participate.

Games

A description of short, cooperative games is included to supplement the session activities. Draw upon these and others you know to introduce movement at appropriate times.

Required Resources

Books

Golenbock, Paul. *Teammates*. New York: Gulliver Books, Harcourt, Brace, Jovanovitch Publishers, 1990.

Hoffman, Mary. *Amazing Grace.* New York: Dial Books for Young Readers, 1991.

Knight, Mary Burns. *Who Belongs Here?: An American Story.* Gardiner, ME: Tillbury House, 1993.

UNICEF Staff. *A Children's Chorus.* New York: E. P. Dutton, 1989.

One of the following books about families:

Adolff, Arnold. *All Colors of the Race.* New York: Lothrop, Lee & Shepard Books, 1992.

Drescher, Joan. *Your Family, My Family.* New York: Walker and Company, 1980.

Simon, Norma. *All Kinds of Families.* Chicago: Albert Whitman and Company, 1976.

Jenness, Aylette. *Families: A Celebration of Diversity, Commitment, and Love.* Boston: Houghton Mifflin Co., 1990.

Songs on Tape

Rainbow People, Susan Stark Music, RR1 Box 77, Canaan, NH 03741

Chicago Children's Choir, 1720 East 54th St., Chicago, IL 60615. Phone (312) ~~324~~-8300. 849 Fax (312) 324-8333

For Background Reference

Wall map of the world, such as the *Peters Projection* World Map (highly recommended)

Chicago Children's Choir Publicity Packet (highly recommended), available from address above.

Materials Needed

Index cards
Yarn
Safety pins
Thick pencils
Crayons, including skin-tone colors
Cassette player
Construction paper in rainbow colors
Tacks or push pins
Glue sticks
Poster board
Newsprint
Cloth sheet or mural paper
Shallow pans
T-pins
Racially inclusive illustrated magazines

Prism
Kaleidoscope
Clear cellophane or mylar
Recycled aluminum pie pans
Magnifying glass(es)
Coffee cans
Duct tape
Flower pots
Plaster of Paris
Tree branches
Baseball cards
Large cardboard box
Wooden dowels
Candle or chalice

Cooperative Games

General

Pull Together

Materials: Long, strong rope.

Description: Divide children into two equal groups so when they pull on the rope as hard as they can, neither side moves.

Special Hints: Switch children so that balance is achieved. When they get the idea that balance is the goal, encourage them to switch themselves.

Blanket Volley Ball

Materials: Blankets, balls.

Description: Players hold the edge of the blanket. A ball is placed on the blanket. The players toss up and try to catch the ball by cooperatively manipulating the blanket.

Variations: Use different sized balls, change blanket size, define boundaries, use a net. Pass ball between two groups.

Special Hints: Switch positions around blanket. Make sure little ones do not get hurt. Help energetic members focus on cooperation.

Standing Together

Game Description: Seated in a circle, players grasp wrists or hands and try to collectively stand up.

Variations: For larger groups; grab people not seated next to each other.

Special Hints: Let the group experiment. Go slowly. The more people, the harder it is.

Rope Raising

Materials: Large rope with the ends tied together tightly.

Description: The group sits in a circle holding the rope with both hands. They then pull all at once and stand.

Variations: Lay rope out in a line and place two equal teams at the ends. Have teams pull together so that everyone stands up.

Special Hints: Coach group to pull together. Watch that the energetic kids do not criticize the less active ones.

Alternate Leaning

Description: Form a circle with arms linked at the elbows. Count off by twos. At the signal, the ones lean in, and the twos lean out. Watch to make sure that the children do not lean too steeply.

Variations: Hold hands, alternate leaning in rhythm.

Special Hints: Keep feet stationary. The more people, the better.

Kid's Carapace

Materials: Blanket or tarp

Description: The group gets on its hands and knees under the blanket (the shell) and tries to move it in one direction.

Variations: Move over an obstacle, act out turtle stories.

Special Hints: Allow the group time to realize that they all need to move in the same direction.

Energy Diffusers

Hop As One

Description: Players stand in a line and lift and extend their left legs so that the person behind can grab their ankle or foot. Players then place right hand on right shoulder of the person in front for support. Now it is hop time!

Variations: Switch legs, do a dance, make circles of players.

Special Hints: Remind them of careful coordination. Practice before getting discouraged.

Pasta

Description: Players are a package of pasta, bundled close (spaghetti works well as an image). As they imagine boiling, players begin to relax and move in waves like boiling spaghetti, eventually ending up in a limp pile on the floor.

Group/Trust Builders

What Does This Mean?

Description: Each player chooses an object that has special value for them. They then share the special value that the object represents for them. For example, a rock represents friendship because of its solidity, or the moon is caring because it lights the earth at night.

Variation: Restrict to natural objects. Agree on one value for group, and have everyone find a different representative object.

Special Hints: Give examples, encourage free expression and leader participation.

Make Me Into You

Description: One player closes eyes and another strikes a sculptured pose. The player whose eyes are closed sculpts a third player into the pose struck by the second, using the sense of touch alone.

Variations: Have a number of players close their eyes and try to duplicate the pose with a partner.

Special Hints: This game brings out the gentleness in people.

Cast Your Vote

Description: Draw a line on the ground (or use an imaginary one) that represents a continuum from "strongly disagree" to "strongly agree." Introduce topics and ask the children to choose a spot on the line that represents how they feel about the issue. No talking.

Special Hints: Do not vote yourself. Include family issues and topics from the curriculum.

Webs

Materials: Ball of yarn or twine

Description: With the group sitting in a circle, have one person hold the end of the twine or yarn, and toss the ball to another. The person holding the ball may speak if they wish to. When they are finished, they hold the yarn and toss the ball to someone else. This continues until the entire group is connected, and the web is formed.

Variations: Have the group address a specific theme.

Special Hints: Allow participants a "pass" option. Play the game regularly to build group identity. Encourage the discussion of difficult and important issues.

Empathy

Chalkboard Drawing

Description: Participants draw circles on chalkboard under various challenging directions, such as with both hands, with the non-dominant hand, blindfolded, or balancing objects on the back of their hands.

Variations: Change shapes or drawing tool, such as holding chalk in a clothespin.

Special Hints: Help the children focus on recognizable shapes.

Resources for Leaders

National Association for the Education of
Young Children
1509 16th Street, N.W.
Washington, DC 20036-1426
(800) 424-2460

Institute of Latin American Studies
Publication Office
Sid Richardson Hall, 1.304
University of Texas at Austin
Austin, TX 78712

Defense for Children International—USA
210 Forsyth Street
New York, NY 10002

John Muir Publications
PO Box 613
Santa Fe, NM 87504

People of Every Stripe
PO Box 12505
Portland, OR 97212
(503) 282-0612

Roots & Wings
Educational Catalog
PO Box 3348
Boulder, CO 80307
(303) 494-1833

Constructive Playthings
1227 E. 119th Street
Grandview, MO 64030
(800) 448-4115
FAX (816) 761-9295

Cooperative Children's Book Center
4290 Helen C. White Hall
University of Wisconsin-Madison
600 N. Park Street
Madison, WI 53706
(608) 263-3720
FAX (608) 262-4933

Zephyr Press
3316 N. Chapel Ave.
PO Box 66006-L
Tucson, Az 85728-6006
(602) 322-5090
FAX (602) 323-9402

Children's Museum of Boston
300 Congress Street
Boston, MA 02210-1034
(617) 426-8855, ext. 287

Glossary

These working definitions from a variety of sources may help leaders, parents, and other adults discuss the concepts of this program.

- **Assimilation.** The policy of forcing cultural groups to adopt the dominant or mainstream culture.
- **Cultural diversity.** Valuing, including, and nurturing a number of distinct cultures. When we say that diversity is a value or goal, we are referring to multiculturalism, not merely tolerating the existence of other cultures.
- **Desegregation.** The abolition of racial segregation.
- **Discrimination.** A legal term that refers to actions of bias or prejudice. Such actions are unethical and illegal.
- **Ethnicity.** From the Greek word *ethnos*, which means company, people, or nation. The term suggests a relationship of kinship, attachment, and ground for self-esteem.
- **Ethnocentrism.** Prejudicial or discriminatory action based on the ethnic origin or identification of an individual or group.
- **Integration.** Coordinating the goals of cultural groups into a uniform society. Historically this has meant putting people together in the hope that diverse cultures will become assimilated into the mainstream culture. A more recent view acknowledges that persons of color can become part of society through meaningful involvement in and power over the decision-making processes that directly affect them.
- **Multiculturalism.** Valuing and nurturing a diversity of cultures within a society.

  Additive multiculturalism: Learning about and taking on the culture of others, thereby expanding the dimensions of mainstream culture.

  Subtractive multiculturalism: Learning about and taking on the dominant culture, thereby becoming assimilated.
- **Pluralism.** The coexistence of many cultures in a given society.
- **Prejudice.** A prejudgment or biased view, feeling, behavior, or action that is rooted more in premature opinion, impression, and stereotype than in social reality. Prejudice is formed without knowledge, considered thought, or the power of reason. Such opinions, feelings, or actions are externalized by individuals within institutions and cultures.
- **Race.** An anthropological term that distinguishes the varieties among the human population based on physical, historical, cultural, national, and geographic particularities. Some anthropologists argue that race is not a legitimate category for humans because it has no biological or scientific basis.
- **Racism.** The US Civil Rights Commission defines racism as any attitude or institutional structure that subordinates a person or group because of his or her color. A popular definition of racism is "prejudice + power = racism."

To be more specific, racism is a social phenomenon designed to isolate, separate, and/or exploit others based on a belief that one racial or ethnic group's identity, physical or cultural characteristics, lifestyle, and aspirations are valuable, normative, and superior while another group's are marginal, subservient, and inferior.

1   The Rights of Every Child

Goals for Participants

- To get to know each other better.
- To understand the rights of all children.
- To be introduced to the concept of racial justice.
- To be introduced to the value of differences.

Background

This session lays a foundation of respect for others by using activities that enhance respect for self. It introduces the concept that all children have the same rights and needs, the concept of racial justice, and the idea that the United States and Canada are countries made up of immigrants from all over the world.

Materials

- A copy of the book *A Children's Chorus.*
- Copies of Handout 1, "Symbols of Children's Rights," Handout 2, "Declaration of the Rights of the Child," and Handout 3, "Body Outlines," for each participant
- Newsprint or poster board
- Two hats or containers
- 4 x 6" index cards
- Large safety pins or yarn
- Pencils
- Crayons, including skin-tone colors
- Felt markers
- Cassette player and *Rainbow People* tape
- World map
- 12 x 18" construction paper
- Glue sticks or paste

Preparation

- Create pair-match name tags by attaching a small picture that represents each word listed below on a separate 4 x 6" card. Leave space to add a child's name on the card. Cut or copy pictures from magazines, or use inexpensive stickers or simple line drawings.

  Use only one picture per card, and use only as many pairs as there are participants. (An adult leader or helper can complete a pair, if necessary.)

  Place the cards depicting objects on the left side of each pair in one container, and all the cards from the right side of each pair in another container.

table	chair
bed	pillow
hand	glove
cup	saucer
ball	bat
soap	towel
stop	go (signs)
hat	head
foot	shoe
knife	fork

- Read the full text of the United Nations 1959 Declaration of the Rights of the Child, found in the back of *A Children's Chorus.* Write the children's version (located in Handout 2) on poster board or newsprint and post it in your meeting space.

- Make a poster of the UU Principles in children's language (below, adapted from *Beginning Unitarian Universalism* by Helena Chapin and Mary Ann Moore) and post next to the Declaration of Rights poster.

Unitarian Universalists believe:

Each person is important.

All people should be treated equally.

Our churches are places where many different people are accepted and where we learn together.

Each person must be free to search for what is true and right in life.

Everyone should have a vote about the things that concern them.

We should work for a peaceful, fair, and free world.

We should care for our planet earth.

- Set up the cassette player and cue the *Rainbow People* tape to the song "All I Really Need." (Also available on the Raffi album, *Baby Beluga*.)

- Post the world map where it can be seen by the group when they are sitting in a circle.

- Gather four or five pictures that represent some of the differences in the human family. Select pictures that help participants see that people come in varied colors and sizes, and live in varied cultures (don't try to select pictures that represent "typical" members of any race).

- If you prefer to make posters for your Focusing activity, make a sample poster to share with the children by cutting apart the rights symbols and pasting them onto a sheet of 12 x 18" construction paper. A copy of Handout 2 could be pasted to the back of the poster.

Session Plan

Arrival

Have the song "All I Really Need" playing as the children arrive. Greet them as they enter and have each one pick a pair-match name tag. Make sure the children select their cards from alternate containers to ensure an even number of matching sets. If necessary, a leader can draw a card to complete a pair.

Be sure you do not have more cards than people, or someone's "match" may not be drawn from the container. Help each child write his or her name on the card and pin it on, or use thick yarn to hang the tag from the neck.

Opening   5 minutes

After the children have received name tags, gather them in a circle on the floor. If you wish, light a candle or chalice in the center of the circle.

Begin introductions by saying your name and one thing you like to do outdoors. Continue in this manner until all have had a chance to introduce themselves. Extinguish the candle.

Focusing   35 minutes

Direct the children's attention to the world map and ask questions to determine if they are familiar with it. Point out the United States or Canada, and ask for the names of other places they know. Briefly describe the countries or regions of origin in your family and point these out on the map.

Ask if any of the children have friends or relatives in another country, or if they know the names of any of the countries from which their parents, grandparents, or great-grandparents came. Continue discussion until the children understand that the world is made up of many countries and peoples.

Say something like, "Our country is made up of people who originally came from all different parts of the world. A long time ago, even before my great-grandparents were born, the people who lived in our country were all from one race. Does anyone know who these first people were?

"Yes, sometimes they're called Indians or Native Americans (or Native Canadians). The great-great-great-grandchildren of these native people still live here, and they are still known as Native Americans (or Native Canadians).

"But, lots of people from all over the world have come and are still coming to this country. All these people from various parts of the world have many differences. They speak different languages. Some of you may have relatives who speak a language different from the one we're using today. People may dress differently from each other. And, they may have different skin colors and features, so we sometimes talk about people of different races." (Introduce the pictures of the human family you've selected to illustrate your point.)

"The Native Americans (or Native Canadians) were the first race of people to live in this country. When other groups, other races, came here they fought with the native people and pushed them from the land they lived on. Most of the Native Americans (or Native Canadians) died. This is one example of how people of one race have been treated unfairly by another race of people. Sadly, one race often treats another race unkindly and unfairly. We have a special name for this—it's called racism. As Unitarian Universalists, we want to learn how to treat all people fairly. Together we're going to learn about racial justice, about treating all people of all races in a way that is fair and right."

Explain that it isn't just the members of our congregation who are concerned with creating a world with racial justice, but that many other groups are trying to work for racial justice, too. Explain that people from all over the world come together at the United Nations seeking a better world, and they have developed a statement about the fair and just treatment of all children all over the world. Read the short declaration posted on the wall. Be sure to relate "black, white, brown, or yellow" to the concept of race. Then read *A Children's Chorus*, which illustrates all the principles.

Distribute Handout 1, markers, and construction paper if making posters. Invite the children to begin coloring in the line drawings as they guess which rights are symbolized by these pictures. Encourage them to draw their own details of clothing, hair, and skin tones on the pictures of people. The 10 rights symbolized by these pictures are listed in Handout 2, with the children's version in the second column. (Please note: When discussing item 5, the preferred meanings of the word "special" are "unusual quality" or "held in particular esteem." For the term "handicapped", substitute phrases like "people with disabilities." Talk about different abilities, not special needs.)

Play the song, "All I Really Need" while children are coloring.

Gather the group in front of the posters of the UN Declaration of Rights of the Child and the UU Principles. Help the children compare and discuss the similarities between the two value statements. Distribute copies of Handout 2 to all the children and tell them they will be able to take their individual posters or illustrations home to finish coloring.

Exploring   10 minutes

Direct the children to find their picture-partner by saying something like, "Look at your name tags. Everyone has a picture that can be matched with a picture on someone else's name tag. Your job now is to find your partner by matching up your name tags in pairs."

When all the pairs have found each other, ask them to sit back-to-back. Distribute pencils, crayons, markers, and Handout 3 (or blank drawing paper if you prefer). Invite the children to draw their partners without looking at them. Encourage them to fill in as many details as they can, such as hair color, eye color, skin tone, clothing, and anything else special about their partners. After a while, tell them that if they run out of memories of their partner to draw from, they can turn around and look at their partners.

While they continue drawing, talk with them about the unique qualities and attributes they all have. Talk about differences in positive terms.

Integration   10 minutes

Ask if anyone had trouble drawing their partners without looking at them. Explain that we may take some differences for granted, like eye color. Some differences we don't notice carefully, like the color of hair or the clothes someone is wearing. But sometimes people are lumped together and treated unfairly because of their differences. Sometimes children are treated unfairly by adults. Sometimes people with lighter skin treat people with darker skin unfairly.

Lead them in a discussion of unfair treatment that arises from differences. Ask them if they have ever been treated unfairly because of how they dress, how they speak, or other differences. Remind them of the UU Principles and the UN

Declaration of Rights of the Child, which both affirm the right of all people to fair, kind, and loving treatment.

Closing   5 minutes

Post the drawings around the room. Form a circle around a candle or a chalice and read the following from the Declaration of Rights of the Child:

"I have the same rights as every child, no matter if I am black, white, brown or yellow, boy or girl; no matter what language I speak, or what my religion is; no matter who my parents are, whether they are rich or poor. I should treat everyone, no matter who they are, as I would want them to treat me: in a way that is fair, friendly, and helpful."

Give the children their posters (or illustrations) with a copy of Handout 2 to take home.

Reflection and Planning

Take a few minutes to reflect on these questions and discuss them with your co-leader.

1. What was good about this session? Why?
2. What was not so good? Why?
3. What can I learn from this session to strengthen future sessions?
4. What do I need to prepare for the next session?

⚫2⚫ What Do You See?

Goals for Participants

- To get to know each other better.
- To find connections with others in the group.
- To understand that people see things differently.
- To feel positive about differences.

Background

This session reinforces a positive attitude toward differences, including differences in abilities and in our perceptions. Listen carefully to hear both positive and negative attitudes toward differences, so that you may reinforce positive attitudes. This session also helps participants learn something about others in the group.

Materials

- Pencils, crayons, and watercolor markers
- Sixteen 9 x 12" sheets of construction paper in four colors
- Tape
- Index cards
- Poster board
- 12 x 18" construction paper for each participant
- Clear plastic laminate (optional)
- Large felt-tip marker
- Cassette player and "Wonderful World" on the *Rainbow People* tape
- Candle or chalice
- Snack

Preparation

- Recruit adult helpers to make and serve a snack.

- Review the song "Wonderful World" and print the refrain on poster board in large letters. If a person with musical talent is available, ask them to come to the first 15 minutes of this session to help teach the song.

- For the UCan Game, cut 16 construction paper circles from four colors (to resemble the floormat in the game Twister®) and lay them out on the floor in a 6 x 6' grid about one-and-a-half to two feet apart. Tape the circles to the floor so that they will not slide. Jot the following actions, and others of your choosing, on an index card:

whistle	wink both eyes
wink one eye	wiggle ears
roll tongue	snap fingers
pat head and	do a cartwheel
rub stomach	swim underwater
stand on head	hop on one foot
jump rope	

- For the What Do You See? activity, create place mats using the sample illustrations at the end of this session to draw several designs on construction paper, one place mat per person.

  For example, draw three circles an inch in diameter, two inches apart on a few pieces of paper. Near the center of others, draw a keyhole two inches high. An oblong shape like a loaf of bread and a large letter Y are other possibilities. Use as many illustrations as needed so that several people have the same design.

Optional: After the children complete their drawings, plan to cover the place mats with clear plastic laminate to make them more permanent.

• Set up the cassette player and cue the tape to the song "Wonderful World."

Session Plan

Arrival

Play "Wonderful World" as the children enter. Draw their attention to the portraits they completed with their partners last week. If you have newcomers, explain that these pictures help us think about the ways we all look just a bit different from everyone else. Ask if any people look exactly alike, and encourage discussion. If someone mentions identical twins, ask them in what ways even identical twins differ from each other (for example, temperament, favorite foods, favorite activities).

Opening   10 minutes

Draw the group into a circle and light the candle or chalice. Teach them the chorus to "Wonderful World." Relate this song to the Declaration of Rights of the Child from Session 1. Explain that today the group will explore some of their differences and similarities.

Focusing: UCan Game   10 minutes

Introduce the UCan Game by directing attention to the circles on the floor. Tell the group that you will call out a part of the body (such as hand, foot, elbow, or knee), a color, and an activity, and they should put that part of their body on that color if they can do that activity. For example, if you say, "Put your hand in red if you can whistle," everyone who can whistle will put one of their hands in a red circle. Remind them to keep their hands on the red circle as they try to do another UCan.

Begin by calling out the first UCan and helping participants respond appropriately. As more UCans are called, the children will become more intertwined. Allow time for participants to enjoy trying to touch all the circles that apply to them simultaneously. Make the point that different people can do different things and that everybody has many wonderful talents.

During the UCan Game, a helper could set up refreshments and lay out the paper place mats and the drawing materials around a table.

Exploring: 20 minutes
What Do You See?

Invite each child to sit in front of a place mat. Say something like, "Each of these place mats has the beginning of a picture on it. What do you see in the design? Complete the picture by drawing and coloring any way you want. Use your imagination to decide how to use the design to make your picture. You can draw lines, color it, write on it, and add anything you want to make your picture."

Look for and encourage children who may have difficulty getting started. Assure them that there is no "right way" to complete the picture. Serve a simple snack while the children work. When the children have finished eating, ask them to help clean up, but leave their place mats in place.

Integrating   10 minutes

Holding up one place mat, ask, "How many of you have a place mat that started with this design?" Call on each child to show and explain what she or he saw in the design. Call attention to how the things they imagined are similar or very different. After all the designs have been shared, discuss other shapes and designs that might have been drawn on any of the place mats. Make the point that when two people look at the same thing, they see something different, and that's okay. Tell the children they may take their place mats home.

Closing   5 minutes

Gather the group in a circle and light the candle or chalice. Say something like, "Today we saw that sometimes we're able to do the same things, and sometimes we're able to do different things. We learned this while we played the UCan Game. Even when we look at a picture, we don't all see the same thing all the time, but we can all be friends and enjoy being together. That's something we have in common. Our differences make us a wonderful group."

Play "Wonderful World" and encourage the children to sing the chorus. With the group holding hands, send a squeeze around the circle. When it comes back, say, "Go in peace" to end the circle.

Reflection and Planning

Take a few minutes to reflect on these questions and discuss them with your co-leader.

1. What was good about this session? Why?
2. What was not so good? Why?
3. What can I learn from this session to strengthen future sessions?
4. What do I need to prepare for the next session?

What Do You See?

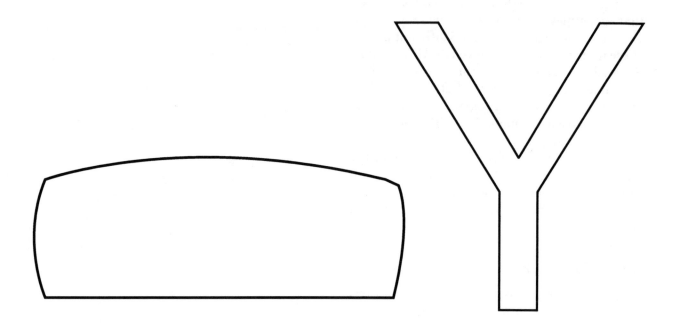

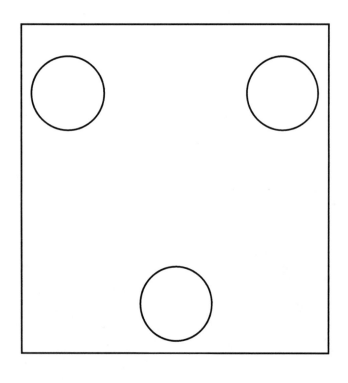

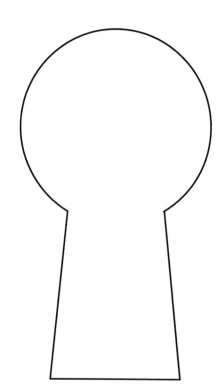

⟨3⟩ We Are All Alike

Goals for Participants

- To explore similarities in the group.
- To discover some of the similarities that children from all backgrounds share.

Background

The first two sessions laid the foundation for our theme—racial justice and cultural inclusivity. In Session 1 we introduced ourselves and the concept of rights. In Session 2 we considered some similarities and differences in our group.

In this session, participants learn more about partners who share common physical characteristics, and also see pictures of many races and ethnic groups in order to reinforce the concept of similarities. Be prepared to discuss people with physical disabilities.

Emphasize the idea of our similarities as human beings without overstating the point and implying that we are all the same. Help the children see that although we are all different (that is, each is unique), we are all similar in important ways, and that everyone is okay just the way they are.

Materials

- Hat or container
- Colored construction paper
- 9 x 12" drawing paper
- Crayons and markers
- A sheet of fabric or a sheet of 4 x 7' paper
- Tempera (water soluble) paint in two colors
- Paint roller pan or shallow foil baking pan
- Pans for wash water
- Towels for drying feet
- Newspapers or drop cloths

- Magazines depicting people from around the world (Be wary of magazines that present people in what is commonly considered exotic national dress. It is important for the children to see images that are realistic, modern, and respectful, rather than stereotypical.)
- Children's scissors, including left-handed scissors
- Cassette player and *Rainbow People* tape
- Copies of Handout 4, "We Come From All Over the World," for each participant
- Snack

Preparation

- Recruit at least one adult helper. The children will be engaged in two separate activities for 15 to 20 minutes and will need adult supervision in both places.

- Cut out pairs of shapes from a variety of colored construction paper. For example, cut two rectangles, one yellow and one red; two circles from blue and green; and two half-moons from white and pink. Make enough pairs of shapes so that all participants will have a partner. Place them in a hat.

- Set up the cassette player and cue the tape to the beginning.

- Divide each piece of drawing paper in half by bisecting it with a dark line. You need one piece for each participant. Lay the papers out on a table, along with crayons and markers.

- Create a banner by laying the 4 x 7' paper or sheet on a washable floor, or on a walk outdoors if possible. Protect the floor with newspapers or a drop cloth under the sheet. Put two pans of tempera paint in two colors and two chairs at one end of the sheet. Place two pans of clean water, two chairs, and towels at the other end.

If you use an old sheet for the banner, consider making it into a rigid hanging for the classroom, the sanctuary, or some other area. To do so, cut the sheet about a foot larger than the finished size. Make a 3 x 6' frame from 1 x 2" lumber. When the banner is dry, stretch the cloth on the frame, stapling the 6" overhang to the back of the frame. Start at the middle of the long side and staple toward the corners. Keep the material taut at all times. Staple the short sides, then turn the corners under and staple them last. Run picture wire across the back of the frame for hanging.

Session Plan

Arrival

Play the tape as the children enter. Greet them as they arrive, and ask them to sit on the floor in a circle.

Opening   10 minutes

Light the candle or chalice. Ask the children to think of something they like to eat. Then say your name and a food you like, and invite everyone to do the same.

Briefly review the previous sessions by saying something like, "A couple of weeks ago we drew pictures of each other trying to remember things about ourselves that are unique—things that no one else has exactly the same—like our special shade of hair or eyes.

"Last week we spent some time sharing our different skills and talents. How many of you can curl your tongue? (Allow children to demonstrate.) How many can rub their stomachs and pat their heads at the same time? Does anyone remember another talent from last week that you can share with us? Now that we've remembered some of our special talents, we're going to think about how we are alike."

Focusing   10 minutes

Shake the hat with the pairs of shapes and invite each child to pick one shape. Ask the group to find the person who has a piece of paper that is like the piece of paper they have.

If the children seem too intent on finding an exact match for their shape, remind them that things that are *alike* do not have to be *exactly* the same, but may differ a little bit. If necessary, tell the children to look for the same shape, not the same color.

When everyone has found a partner, ask, "How are these paper cutouts the same, and how are they different?" Listen to all of their responses, then reinforce the idea that something can be alike in some ways and different in others.

Ask the partners to sit next to each other at the table where the paper and markers are laid out. Say something like, "Now that we all have partners, we are going to look at our partners and think of ways that we are alike." Ask one child at a time to name something they have in common with their partner. Physical similarities may be what they notice first—for example, two eyes, ten fingers, or brown hair.

Solicit other ways in which partners are alike. They may share abilities like walking, running, or swimming. They may have similar hair color or wear a similar style of clothes. They may have shared interests, such as soccer or playing with dolls. Expand the discussion to include emotions: All have been happy, angry, or sad at one time or another; this is another likeness that people share. Help them find similarities if they don't immediately see them.

Say something like, "We have a lot in common. We are alike in many ways. We have faces, hands, and mouths; we breathe, talk, walk, eat, and play. We come to this church. We can be sad, mad, or glad—we all share that, though we don't all have the same feelings at the same time. Now we are going to make another kind of drawing of something we have in common: our hands. How are our hands alike?" (They have fingers. They have palms with lines in them. They have ridges on the fingertips or fingerprints.)

Help the children trace an outline of each partner's hand onto one side of their papers.

Everyone should end up with an outline of their own hand on one side of their paper, and their partner's hand on the other side. When they are done, ask, "Is your hand exactly the same as your partner's hand? How is it alike? How is it different?"

Summarize by saying, "We are alike in many ways. But that doesn't mean that we should all be exactly the same, or that we should want to be exactly like each other. We can enjoy being alike without having to wish we were all the same. Because our hands are alike we can do similar things, like play ball together and eat together, so we're very glad to have them. But our hands aren't exactly the same, and they don't have to be. Some hands are bigger than others, some fingers are longer than others. We can enjoy our hands just as they are."

Exploring   20 minutes

Introduce the next activity by saying, "Now we are all going to make a banner with another part of our bodies that is alike: our feet."

Explain that everyone will have a turn to come over, take off their shoes and socks, dip their feet in paint, and make footprints on the banner. Tell the children that the foot banner will hang on the wall when it's dry.

Bring out the magazines and explain that while people are waiting their turn to make footprints, they will be cutting out pictures of people from all over the world who are like us in many ways.

With adult supervision, start the children cutting out pictures while they take turns, two at a time, making footprints. Have two children step into the basins of paint at one end, walk the length of the sheet, and sit down at the other end to wash and dry their feet. Repeat the process for all the children. (If the sheet is paper, the paint may be slippery; have adult helpers walk along holding the children's hands.)

Serve the snack as the children cut out pictures.

Integrating   10 minutes

When you have finished printing the banner, gather the group and turn their attention to the pictures they have been cutting out. Point out that these people—like the paper shapes participants used to find partners today—come in many different colors.

Discuss how the people in these pictures are similar to the children. Ask, "Do they do things that are like the things we do? Are their feelings like ours?" Use the pictures to illustrate any similarities already discussed. Collect the pictures to use in the next session.

Introduce the theme for next week by saying something like, "Because we live in the United States (Canada), I can guess that most of us have relatives who came here from another country or part of the world. This week I want you to talk with your family about the different parts of the world your family comes from, so next week we can find all our different countries on the map."

Distribute copies of Handout 4.

Closing   5 minutes

If the children need a movement activity, lead them in a game selected from the list on page 7.

If a quiet closing seems more appropriate, have the children form pairs around the circle and show them how to play Mirrors in silence. Each pair chooses one partner to be the mirror. The pairs maintain eye contact while the mirror copies everything the other person does—every movement of the face and body. If they concentrate and move slowly, the movements will seem to happen at exactly the same time. After one minute has passed, ask the partners to switch roles and continue for one more minute.

Gather in a circle holding hands around the candle or chalice. Ask one child to send a squeeze "around the world." When the squeeze comes back to the one who started it, she or he can say, "Go in peace."

Remind the children to take their hand prints and Handout 4 home.

Reflection and Planning

Take a few minutes to reflect on these questions and discuss them with your co-leader.

1. What was good about this session? Why?
2. What was not so good? Why?
3. What can I learn from this session to strengthen future sessions?
4. What do I need to prepare for the next session?

Send copies of Handout 4 to the families of any children who were absent today. Follow-up phone calls will increase the number of responses for the next session.

4 We Are All Different

Goals for Participants

- To share their differences.
- To gain an understanding that differences are positive.

Background

In past sessions, children have shared who they are, got to know each other better, and worked with others in the group. They have found that they share common characteristics with each other and with others in the world. This session deals with differences, stressing positive diversity.

Materials

- Footprint banner from Session 3
- Two copies of Handout 5, "Cornucopia," for each participant
- Crayons or water-soluble markers
- Cassette player and *Rainbow People* tape
- People pictures from Session 3
- Masking tape or thumbtacks
- Poster board
- Colored string or thread, preferably a different color for each participant
- Pushpins
- World map
- Snack

Preparation

- Supplement the people pictures that the children cut out in Session 3 with additional pictures. Be sure to collect a variety of pictures of people with different racial backgrounds to represent the United States and Canada. Note the country of origin on the back of each picture. Look for contemporary, not exotic, depictions.

- Post the world map on a bulletin board or mounting board, so that pushpins may be used. Leave an 8 to 10" border around the map.

- Familiarize yourself with the melody of the song "He's Got the Whole World in His Hands." You will be singing it with revised words.

- Arrange for a snack of very colorful foods, such as purple grape juice, carrot sticks, and cookies frosted with tinted icing.

Session Plan

Arrival

Play the tape *Rainbow People* as the children arrive. Greet the children and collect their family histories.

Opening and Focusing   10 minutes

Invite the children to sit in a circle around the candle or chalice. Remind participants what they did last week. Say something like, "Last week we talked about some of the characteristics that we share. What are some ways that we are alike?"

Show the banner created last week and ask, "Who can tell us how we made this?" Lead a short discussion of their footprint art, inviting them to try to find their own footprints, and review the similarities.

Draw the children's attention to the pictures they cut out during the last session. Spread the pictures on the floor or on a table and ask them to look for differences in hair, eyes, skin, facial features, and clothing. Some of the pictures may also show differences in written language, geography, etc.

Help the children identify many differences, then lead a discussion of the differences present in the room. Conclude by saying something like: "All human beings are alike in some ways, and all humans differ in some ways. Both our similarities and our differences are a part of being human."

Exploring   20 minutes

Distribute one copy of Handout 5 to each participant. Give each child only one crayon, all of the same color. Invite everyone to color the picture in front of them.

When they have finished, give each child a second copy of Handout 5. This time let them use all the colors of crayons and markers available to color this drawing.

Have the children take turns holding up their pictures to share with the class, or post all the same color pictures together and all the multi-colored pictures together. Encourage reactions by saying something like, "Are there some pictures you like better than others? What makes them more interesting?"

Some children may respond that the one-color pictures are boring, dull, or "unreal." Someone may have used patterns of stars, stripes, or dots to create a picture that may be more interesting than some of the multicolored pictures. If so, point out that the variety of patterns took the place of a variety of colors. Suggest that a variety of colors and patterns is more pleasing than just one color or pattern.

Say something like, "We can say the same of people and many other things in our lives. If everybody and everything were green, it might be interesting at first, but it could get dull and boring very quickly. Look around you and think green. Imagine that everything in this room is green, everything in your home is green. Everything you see is green. All your meals are green,

from chicken to potato chips and everything in between. I don't know about you, but I would soon get very tired of the color green."

Gather the group in a circle around the world map. Point out that people come in a variety of colors, and that they live and dress differently all over the world. Spend a few minutes acquainting the group with the map.

Talk about the differences in the human family. Post the people pictures from Session 3 around the map, pointing out the countries where those people live.

Conclude by saying something like, "All the colors of people—red, black, brown, white, and yellow—are beautiful. Different people in different parts of the world may look and dress differently, depending on where they live. Inuits wear heavier clothes, sometimes made out of fur. They live in cold climates. Africans wear lighter clothes, often made out of cotton.

"People all over the world live according to the climate and customs in their home country. We wear different clothes for different seasons of the year. A bathing suit is good for a hot summer day, but not for a cold day in the middle of winter."

Invite discussion.

Integrating   20 minutes

Ask the children to stand, join hands, and move in a circle while you teach them a song sung to a tune from our African-American heritage, "He's Got the Whole World in His Hands." Sing these two verses:

We've got the whole world on our map.
(repeat 3 more times)

We've got the whole world in our thoughts.
(repeat 3 more times)

Sit in a circle again. Explain that some of the children in the group have family members or ancestors who come from other countries. Say something like, "We agreed last week to find out something about where our families came from. Now we are going to put ourselves and our families on the map, so we can see where we're all from. As I call your name, come to the map. We will stretch a colored string from your name to the places your family comes from."

When the children have finished marking their families' countries of origin, discuss the results. Say something like, "We have come from all over the world. Our map looks like a web—a web that ties us all together as a diverse community. I'm glad that we are together here, so that we can share our stories with each other."

Closing   5 minutes

Have the group stand in a circle. Light the candle or chalice. Invite the children to hold hands and move in a circle as they sing two more verses to the tune of "He's Got the Whole World in His Hands."

> We've got families on our map.
> (repeat 3 more times)

> We've got families in our thoughts.
> (repeat 3 more times)

Say something like, "Today we talked about how differences make the world more interesting, make foods more attractive, help us appreciate other people, and make our world a better place. Let's enjoy the different colors in our snack today." Share the snack, and remind everyone to take their colored pictures home.

Reflection and Planning

Take a few minutes to reflect on these questions and discuss them with your co-leader.

1. What was good about this session? Why?
2. What was not so good? Why?
3. What can I learn from this session to strengthen future sessions?
4. What do I need to prepare for the next session?

⑤ Families Come in All Shapes and Sizes

Goals for Participants

- To grow in awareness and appreciation of the diversity of families.

Background

Each week we have learned more about ourselves and our group. We are aware of our specialness, our similarities, and our differences. We have explored our family origins. This week we will introduce our families.

Many children have two parents and siblings who share the same biological parents. Some may have step siblings. Some may have adopted brothers or sisters, or may themselves be adopted, perhaps with parents of different races. Some may come from lesbian or gay families.

There will probably be a wide diversity in the composition of families in your group, but if not, be sure to include gay and lesbian families, multiracial families, and adoptive families in your discussion. Introducing children to a variety of families in a matter-of-fact, affirming manner will help them think of all families as "normal" and fully within the bounds of the term "family."

Session 4 helped us become aware of how diversity makes for beauty. We affirmed that, with their many differences, people everywhere are endowed with intelligence, beauty, and all the attributes of being human. This session affirms the beauty of diversity in our families.

Materials

- Crayons in all skin tones
- Pencils
- Drawing paper
- Poster board or bulletin board (optional)
- Paste, tape, or pushpins
- A copy of one of the following books (see Required Resources):
  Your Family, My Family by Joan Drescher
  All Kinds of Families by Norma Simon
  Families: A Celebration of Diversity, Commitment, and Love by Aylette Jenness
  All Colors of the Race by Arnold Adolff
- Snack
- Cassette player and *Rainbow People* tape

Preparation

- Cue the *Rainbow People* tape to the song "All I Really Need." "All I Really Need" is also available on the Raffi album, *Baby Beluga.*

- Cut the drawing paper into large circles, or draw the outline of a large circle on each piece of paper.

- Be prepared to paste on posterboard the family pictures that the children will draw, or attach them to a wall or bulletin board.

- Prepare a snack.

Session Plan

Arrival

As the children arrive, direct their attention to the world map. Invite newcomers to observe the strings indicating where the group's ancestors came from. Collect any additional information sheets and add them to the map display.

Say something like, "We come from many places in the world. We bring our family stories together to this place with love and appreciation."

Opening   5 minutes

Gather the group in a circle and light the candle or chalice. Ask the children, "What is a family?" Welcome all contributions.

Look for opportunities to make this concept more and more inclusive: "Families can include friends. Families can include children who come together when their parents come together to make a home. A family can be people who live together and care about each other. But not all families live in the same home."

Encourage discussion. Explore what the children know about different kinds of families: two-parent, one-parent, multiracial, extended, adopted, blended, gay or lesbian, etc. Affirm the rightness of all "sizes and shapes" of families.

Focusing   15 minutes

Read one of the books about the diversity of families. Invite further discussion about the differences in the children's own families or in other families they know.

If you choose *Families* by Aylette Jenness, read one or two of the stories and show all the pictures. Ask each time, "Is this a family?" Lead the children in answering, "Yes!"

To focus on multiracial families, use *All the Colors of the Race*, a collection of poems about a girl whose mother is black and Christian and whose father is white and Jewish. Read the poems "I am," "all three," "flavors," "I am making a circle for myself," and any others you think the children would enjoy.

Exploring   25 minutes

Pass out pencils, crayons, and the prepared drawing paper. Say something like, "We all know each of us is different in some ways from everyone else in this room, and that in some ways we are all alike. Families are like that, too. Every family is different, yet all families are alike in

some ways. Let's look at our families . . ."

Ask the children to draw and color their families in the circle. Suggest that they start by drawing themselves, then everyone else who is in their family. Invite them to add as much detail as they wish.

Encourage discussion about who is in their families: parents or other adults who take care of them, brothers and sisters, grandparents, aunts, friends, pets, and so on.

Encourage the children to draw in facial features and other identifying physical characteristics, such as raspberry marks, braces, glasses, or wheelchairs. Allow time for coloring such details as skin color, hair, and clothes.

Integrating   5 minutes

Post the children's pictures. Invite discussion about each child's place in his or her family group. Ask, "What is it like to be oldest? Youngest? In the middle? A single child?"

Be aware of and affirm racial and other diversities in families. Say, "We come from many kinds of families. Some are large and some are small. Some have one parent and some have two. Real families come in different sizes and shapes and colors."

Closing   5 minutes

Gather in a circle and light the candle or chalice. Say something like, "We shared our families, and we talked about some of the different kinds of families we know, and some families we haven't met. All our families *can* provide us with the love and understanding we need to grow up strong and healthy. That's the great thing about families: that all kinds of families can give us what we need."

Play the song "All I Really Need" and demonstrate simple hand movements to correspond to "song in my heart," "food in my belly," and "love in my family." Invite the children to add these movements to the song as they sing it.

Reflection and Planning

Take a few minutes to reflect on these questions and discuss them with your co-leader.

1. What was good about this session? Why?
2. What was not so good? Why?
3. What can I learn from this session to strengthen future sessions?
4. What do I need to prepare for the next session?

6 Color From the Rainbow

Goals for Participants

- To experience how individual efforts contribute to the making of a whole.
- To think about the human race as the rainbow race.

Background

This session uses the rainbow concept to emphasize the coming together of separate, distinct entities to make one complete and beautiful whole.

Materials

- A long blade of grass (optional)
- White paper, at least 44 x 60"
- Copies of Handout 6, "Human Figures," for each participant
- Poster paint OR construction paper in red, orange, yellow, green, blue, indigo, and violet
- Paintbrushes and sponges, one aluminum pie pan (preferably reused), smocks, bowls of clean water, and towels for each participant OR scissors and glue
- Clear cellophane wrap on a frame
- Prism (optional)
- Kaleidoscope (optional)
- Snack

Preparation

- Collect and display around the room pictures of rainbows, nature, children's faces, and a diversity of people.

- Read "The Gift of Color" (located at the end of this session) and prepare to tell rather than read it.

- Stretch a piece of cellophane over a cardboard or wooden frame to illustrate what the world looked like before there was any color. A prism to generate a spectrum will increase the impact of the story.

- Before the session, you may want to paint the large sheet of paper with a blue watercolor wash. To do so, mix a small amount of blue paint with a large amount of water and brush or sponge it onto the paper. Allow it to dry thoroughly before the session.

- Make an arc on the paper, using a pencil and string as a large compass.

- Use Handout 6 as a template to cut one or more sponges into the shape of a human figure. One sponge can be used to print several colors of paint if you rinse it out between printings.

- If you decide to use construction paper instead of paint, each child will use the template to cut out two or more figures in each of the seven colors to paste along the arc of the rainbow. In that case, you need not prepare the sponges.

Session Plan

Arrival

Greet the children as they arrive and direct their attention to the pictures of rainbows and people displayed in the room.

Opening   5 minutes

Gather the children in a circle and light the candle or chalice. Say something like, "Today we are going to think about rainbows. Who has seen a rainbow?" Encourage discussion by asking, "Who can tell us what a rainbow is? When can we see a rainbow? What colors are in a rainbow? How many colors are in a rainbow?" If appropriate, share the following information about rainbows:

> The rainbow is known all over the world by many names. Italians call it "the flashing arch." In Sanskrit, it is "the bow of Indra." The people of Annam call a rainbow "the little window in the sky." North African tribes greet the rainbow as "the bride of the rain." In the various languages of central Europe, the rainbow is called "the arch of Saint Martin," "the bridge of the Holy Spirit," "the crown of Saint Bernard," and "the girdle of God."
> —Walter J. Saucier,
> *World Book*,
> Field Enterprises, 1971

Focusing   5 minutes

Ask if anyone can think of stories they have heard about rainbows. Then say something like, "People all over the world have stories about rainbows. Some people say there's a pot of gold at the end of the rainbow. They say if you could ever find the place, very far away, where it touches the ground, you would find that pot of gold and be rich. That story comes from the Irish.

"Jewish people tell a story about the rainbow, too. They say the rainbow is a sign, a promise from their God that the world will never be destroyed. They say the rainbow first appeared after a great, angry flood that nearly destroyed everything. When they see the rainbow they know their God is keeping a promise made long ago.

"I'm going to tell you another story about the rainbow, and this one will help us to understand the world better. You'll see what I mean when we get to the end of the story."

Exploring   10 minutes

Tell the story "The Gift of Color," located at the end of this session.

Integrating: 30 minutes
The People Rainbow

Gather the children around the large sheet of paper as you begin to discuss the story. Let the children play with the prism and make their own rainbows. Lead a discussion of the value of color in our lives.

Say something like, "Today we are going to build a people rainbow. Sometimes the human race is also called the Rainbow Race. Do you know why?

"Yes, it's because people come in so many colors. You can see by holding your hand next to someone else's that no two skin tones are exactly alike. And you can see from all the beautiful pictures we've collected for our map that real people come in a wide variety of colors.

"Like the people in the story, all real people have some color or we wouldn't be able to see them. We are going to make a big poster to hang in our church to remind all of us, adults and children alike, that we're proud to be part of the Rainbow Race."

Have the children use Handout 6 to cut figures from the various colors of construction paper and paste them along the arc on the paper. Or, if you're using paint, set out the pie pans and fill each with a color of poster paint. Have participants don smocks and use a paintbrush to apply color to one side of a sponge, the press the sponge lightly to the paper. Rinse out the sponge before using the next color, unless you have a sponge for each color.

Closing   10 minutes

Gather the group in a circle and light the candle or chalice. Hold up the kaleidoscope and ask, "Who can tell me what this is? What will we see when we look through it?" Pass it around. Allow time for reactions. Say something like, "What did you see? Can you name the colors? How is the kaleidoscope like our rainbow?" Encourage discussion about the colors coming together in special ways.

Then say, "Together we made a beautiful rainbow. Many people see our country as a rainbow—many different people from many different places, people of different colors and backgrounds, coming together to make one colorful whole."

Take a few moments to give thanks for the rainbows that color our lives. Invite each child to name a color he or she is glad to be able to see, and why. For example, "I'm glad I can see black; it's the color of my cat." "I'm glad to see light coffee-brown; that's the color of my best friend's skin."

Reflection and Planning

Take a few minutes to reflect on these questions and discuss them with your co-leader.

1. What was good about this session? Why?
2. What was not so good? Why?
3. What can I learn from this session to strengthen future sessions?
4. What do I need to prepare for the next session?

The Gift of Color

by Robin Gray

This story is new. It was written for you.

Imagine a time long ago when things were just getting started. The first flowers were blooming; the first birds were building their nests high in the branches of sheltering trees; girls and boys, men and women setting up their first families and homes. These are the things that you might have seen if it wasn't so dark. No one could see, because it was the first night, and the first day hadn't happened yet.

The First People could hear the wind whining in the trees, and the birds twittering and whistling. It was so dark they couldn't see anything, but the First People were too busy to worry about the dark. They were thinking about all the first things they would need to live beyond that first night. The First People were working so hard that they really didn't care that they couldn't see each other in the dark. As they spoke, they would turn their bodies toward sounds of voices that didn't have faces.

When the sun finally rose on that first morning, the whole world looked like it was made of glass. [Show the cellophane wrap on the frame.] One by one the First People realized they still couldn't see anything. Their faces and muscles and bones were all clear. Light passed straight through their bodies to the clear ground below. The sky was clear. The trees, birds, flowers, and rocks were all as clear as glass.

Finally, one of the First Children broke the silence. "I have eyes to see with," the child cried. "But there's nothing to see!" One of the adults tried to comfort the child, but the First People were all sad.

"What will we do?" one woman said. "Last night we planned to gather the tall grass that rustles in the breeze. We planned to bend and fold, and twist and tie that grass to make the first baskets. Then, we were going to go down to the river, which we hear moving past us, to collect baskets full of water, so all the First People could have a drink."

"Oh-hh-hh," moaned a thirsty man. "How will you find the grass if you can't see it? How will you know if you've made a tight basket if you can't see your work? How will you find your way to the water and back?"

The First People were very creative and solved all these problems, one by one. Holding hands, they formed a human chain to make a trail to the tall grass. They took small, careful steps, never knowing when clear grass might give way to clear rocks or clear tree stumps. Once the human chain was finally in place, the person on the end felt carefully for one long, thick blade of grass, pulled it out of the ground and passed it to the next person, who passed it to the next, until the blade of grass reached the last person in line. [You could have the children close their eyes and pass a long blade of grass around the circle.]

After the grass had been plucked, several First People started weaving baskets, feeling their work with their fingers to find even the tiniest holes that would let water out. Finally they had a few baskets that could hold water. Once again all the First People formed a human chain and worked their way to the river. When a basket was passed to the last man in line, he dipped it carefully into the river he couldn't see and pulled it up full of water. The First People breathed a sigh of relief when the man shouted, "It's holding! It's holding!" And so it was that the First People shared their first drink of water.

The First People had been hard at work all day, and they'd only accomplished one thing—getting a drink! Although the First People had plenty to drink, they had nothing to eat, and they all went to sleep hungry.

When the sun came up again, nothing had changed, except the First People were more worried about how to take care of themselves in a world where nothing could be seen. As the day passed, the First Women and Men planned ways to collect food. A First Child who was playing found something hard—a rock, a crystal-clear rock. She tossed the rock up in the air and it twinkled in the sun. The child held it up for her mother to see. Stretching out her clear arm, with the clear rock in her clear hand, something happened. Stripes of something not-clear showed on her face and reflected on the ground below. [Demonstrate with a prism.]

When the girl's mother saw the stripes of something not-clear, she called the others around. The First People were excited as they felt on the ground for more clear stones that would make those seven wonderful not-clear stripes. The girl's mother decided to name the stripes. Pointing to each in turn she called out, "Red! Orange! Yellow! Green! Blue! Indigo! Violet!" The First People played with the stripes until the sun set.

On the third morning, a gentle rain fell. The First People set out their baskets to catch the rain and talked again about how to gather food. They almost didn't notice when the rain stopped and the sun came out. Looking up, the First People saw above them the same not-clear stripes they had played with the day before: red, orange, yellow, green, blue, indigo, and violet. As the sun grew brighter, the stripes glowed stronger.

Suddenly one man said, "What if we take our baskets and form a line to the stripes? Can we bring the red, orange, and yellow home? Can we pass green and blue, indigo and violet down the line, and use the stripes to make our world not-clear?"

No one knew the answers, but everyone was willing to try. They formed a human chain so long it led straight to the stripes in the sky. At the head of the line was the woman who had named the stripes. She filled the baskets and passed them back down the line. As she turned with the last basket full of violet, the First People gasped. All the beautiful colors were dripping out of the baskets! But the groans soon turned to cheers, for when the very first drop fell to the earth, it colored a flower a brilliant shade of red. The next drop caught a bird's wing in flight. The whole world came alive in shades of red, orange, yellow, green, blue, indigo, and violet. Trees appeared, and blue and yellow mingled to color the grasses green.

The First People were so busy watching their world change that they almost forgot that *they* were still as clear as glass. Suddenly a man tossed his basket of indigo high overhead and ran down the line of First People to await the shower of color below. Others followed his lead. Soon all the First People were playing with the colors falling from the sky. They rolled in the green grass and hugged gray tree trunks. They chased orange butterflies and marveled at purple flowers. All the colors were still quite wet, and a bit of each rubbed off on everybody. When the colors finally dried, the First People found that *they* were all different colors. Some were warm, dark brown like the earth. Others were the color of honey, or shades of rose and burnished bronze mingled together. Some were pink all over, and others were touched by the yellow of the sun and golden buttercups.

They were thankful for this blessing of color. Now they could see the color of ripe apples and the blush of juicy peaches, and gather good food to eat. They could see the river run, birds fly, and fish swim. They could walk with their heads held high, their eyes seeking the best path. And they could learn from everything they could see.

When they looked at each other and saw all the beautiful colors of the First People, they were especially happy, and never wanted to be in a world without color again.

⁷ A Look at Stereotyping

Goals for Participants

- To identify the uniqueness of individual members of a category.
- To explore the concept of stereotyping.

Background

Our world is so complex that we tend to categorize the elements of our environment to make it easier to comprehend. This tendency to generalize and categorize sometimes leads us to stereotype other people and to forget that each person is unique. Stereotypes applied to people can limit each person's ability to become fully themselves. Thus, even though putting similar entities into categories has its purpose, it also has a potential to harm.

As a prelude to discussing the ways people stereotype other people, children will look at some examples of unique living forms and consider how we tend to categorize them. Children will examine several groups of things that appear to be "all alike", such as leaves from the same tree or animals of the same species. They will understand that once we know that an oak leaf or an aspen leaf fits a particular pattern, we can pick out other oak leaves and aspen leaves by fitting the new leaf into a category of leaves with similar characteristics.

However, if we collect several examples of any one type of leaf or animal, it is easy to see that a close examination reveals the differences in each one. Leaves and many animals offer excellent examples of the stereotypes or categories of likeness that we apply to all the members of a group. They also show us how the individual members of any group are unique and individual.

During the Integrating activity, the unique properties of tree branches will be highlighted with paint to reinforce the concept that every member of every group is unique and deserves to be treated as an individual. In addition, a wonderful story, *Amazing Grace*, will help the children apply these concepts to their lives, and discuss their own experiences.

Materials

- Vase or flowerpot
- Newsprint and markers or blackboard and chalk
- Pictures of common animals, such as squirrels, dogs, and cats
- Magnifying glass
- 6" plastic pots or empty coffee cans, one for each participant
- Tree branches about 2" in diameter, one for each participant
- Plaster of Paris
- Cassette player and *Rainbow People* tape
- Water-soluble paints in many colors
- Paintbrushes
- Smocks
- Newspaper or drop cloths
- Water and towels
- A copy of the book *Amazing Grace* by Mary Hoffman (see Required Resources)
- Snack

Preparation

- Collect many leaves or flowers of one type—for example, oak leaves or chrysanthemums. Have at least a half dozen examples to illustrate the diversity of each category.

  If you have the time and the appropriate

environment, you can plan on taking the children outside to collect leaves and flowers at the beginning of the session. Or find good, clear photographs of animals that show several individuals in a group, such as litters of cats, dogs, or wild animals.

Study the photos to familiarize yourself with differences such as size, coloration, and markings.

- Collect and trim tree branches to stand about 2 to 2 1/2' tall. Select branches that have a fairly thick single stem. Place each branch in a 6" flower pot or coffee can and secure with plaster of Paris. Let dry.

- Collect the paints, paintbrushes, water bucket, old towels, and painting shirts or smocks.

- Read *Amazing Grace*.

- If you plan to take the children outside, enlist an adult to stay in the room to greet latecomers.

Session Plan

Arrival

Play the *Rainbow People* tape as the children arrive. Direct their attention to the leaf or picture collection.

Opening   5 minutes

Gather the children in a circle and light the candle or chalice. Invite everyone to say what their favorite color is today, and why.

Focusing: Focus on Plants   10 minutes

If you plan to use samples from outdoors, explain to the children that they will spend a few minutes outside collecting leaves and flowers. Review places where leaves and flowers might be readily found. Be sure that all the children are appropriately dressed before you leave, and have an adult stay behind to greet and direct late

arrivals. Also be sure to show the children what they can and cannot pick or pick up. Allow about five minutes to collect materials.

When the children have collected materials, or you have brought out the materials you brought to the session, ask the children to group the materials by "likeness."

Briefly discuss how we recognize each individual object as a member of a larger category. Ask each child to select two examples of the same specimen (for example, two oak leaves). Say, "We know that these are both oak leaves, but are they exactly the same? How are they different?"

Let the children name differences, such as size, pattern, and coloring. Let them examine the specimens with a magnifying glass.

Help the children understand that although it is important to be able to categorize plants or other living things by the characteristics they share, it is even more important to remember that each individual is unique. Set the flowers and stems in the vase, and arrange the leaves around the base of the vase.

Or Focus on Animals

If you're focusing on animals and using pictures, your discussion may be more like this:

Gather the group around the newsprint or chalkboard and ask them to tell you how to recognize a squirrel (or other animal familiar to them). Write their answers on the newsprint or chalkboard. For a squirrel, you might have a list that reads: gray, fur, long tail, four legs, climbs trees, sits on haunches to eat, likes nuts.

Ask if all squirrels are exactly alike. Help the group to consider that some squirrels have longer tails than others. After eliciting a few answers, summarize by saying, "Some squirrels have just a bit of brown in their fur, and others seem to have a lot of brown. Some squirrels are black. Some squirrels might prefer some kinds of nuts to others, just as some pets prefer different foods." Use pictures to illustrate the differences.

Explain that even though we think of squirrels as being furry, gray animals with long tails, each squirrel is unique; no two squirrels are exactly alike. Show the pictures you collected and elicit the children's ideas of how the animals are different from each other even though they are all dogs, cats, or rabbits. Ask if any one has two pets of the same type, for instance, two dogs, two cats, or two rabbits. Find out if the animals have unique likes and dislikes, habits or behaviors. Help the children understand that although it's important to be able to categorize plants and animals by the characteristics they share, it's even more important to remember that each individual is unique.

Exploring: Amazing Grace   15 minutes

Discuss how people are sometimes categorized in a similar fashion. Say, "Sometimes people put other people into categories, too. When they do that, they ignore the uniqueness of each person. You might hear people say things like, 'Of course she has red hair, she's Irish,' or even, 'Asian-American children always do well in math and science.'

"When you hear someone saying something that's supposed to be true of a whole group of people, you should stop and think. Suppose someone said to you, 'All boys play baseball.' What would you think? Do you know of boys who don't play baseball? Suppose someone said, 'Girls don't play baseball.' Is that true? Do you know of any girls who play baseball?"

Invite discussion of any experiences the children have had with stereotyping—that is, being put in a category and not appreciated for their uniqueness. Read the book *Amazing Grace* to the children, showing them the wonderful illustrations. Help the children understand the connection between stereotyping people and the story, and how stereotyping limits people and is unfair.

Integrating: Painting Trees   20 minutes

Bring out the potted tree limbs and ask the children how the branches are different. They might observe differences in size, color, texture, knots, or shape. Give each child a branch and explain that they will have a chance to decorate their tree branch according to its unique properties. The designs they paint will be different because all the branches are different.

Have the children don smocks. Explain that in Mexico store owners hire artists to paint their trees with designs that show what kind of store stands behind the tree. The artists try to make patterns that bring out the unique shape of the tree. They put lines at different angles, or start painting around a knot and work their way out from there. Ask the children to consider their branches carefully and imagine what design might suit their unique branch. Have a snack available as the children work.

Closing   5 minutes

Gather the group in a circle and light the candle or chalice. Invite the children to show their decorated branches. Ask how each design fits that particular branch. Point out the differences in the designs, and the way they enhance the particular characteristics of the branch. Tell them the painted branch will be their reminder that every plant, animal, and person is unique and deserves individual attention.

For the next session, invite the children to bring in some baseball cards if they wish, because they will hear a true baseball story.

Reflection and Planning

Take a few minutes to reflect on these questions and discuss them with your co-leader.

1. What was good about this session? Why?
2. What was not so good? Why?
3. What can I learn from this session to strengthen future sessions?
4. What do I need to prepare for the next session?

8 ⦂ A Look at Prejudice

Goals for Participants

- To explore the concepts of prejudice and racism and understand that racial prejudice is wrong.
- To share their own experiences with prejudice.
- To learn that prejudging limits our experiences and growth.

Background

Previous sessions have laid a foundation for understanding racial justice. This session addresses prejudice—the pre-judging that arises from ignorance, misunderstanding, and fear.

We suggest that co-leaders review the Introduction and meet to talk candidly about their feelings and perceptions, particularly in regard to talking with children about racism and its effects. We realize that in some ways this topic may be more difficult for adults than for children.

This session emphasizes that prejudice prevents people from getting to know others with different backgrounds, talents, and gifts to bring to the community. This session also promotes the belief that the human community is enriched by racial and ethnic diversity and is diminished by homogeneity. It stresses that prejudice is unfair and ultimately hurts everyone. When we allow our prejudices to keep us apart from other people, we all lose. Without a variety of cultures and experiences, our society would be less interesting and less capable of meeting future challenges.

Materials

- A copy of the book *Teammates* (see Required Resources)
- Copies of Handout 7, "The Rainbow Team," for each participant
- Drawing paper
- Crayons in a variety of skin tones
- Bowls of water and towels for washing
- A snack that includes Ugli fruit or some other unusual but tasty fruit, such as kiwi, pomegranate, jicamo, or prickly pear
- Cassette player and *Rainbow People* tape
- Baseball cards

Preparation

- Meet with teachers and helpers to discuss feelings and thoughts about the topics of prejudice and racism.

- In leading discussions and activities in this session, be guided by the racial composition of your congregation and neighborhood. Two scripts are provided in the focusing section—one for racially diverse groups and one for racially homogeneous groups. Be prepared to talk about a current news event or local situation to illustrate the concept of prejudice.

  Often, children of this age can readily describe their experience with prejudice, although they need concrete examples to make a connection to their own lives. Be ready to tell a personal story of an experience you have had with prejudice to encourage discussion and sharing.

- Learn the song "We've Got the Whole World" from the *Rainbow People* tape and be prepared to lead it.

- In this session, the snack is a learning experience. Ugli fruit can be found at most supermarkets. It is a tired-looking, rough-skinned fruit in the citrus family, about the size of a grapefruit, with a greenish-yellowish-brownish-puckered peel. If possible, buy enough Ugli fruit so that each participant can take one home at the end of the session. Ugli fruit works best for this activity, but you can substitute other unusual and unattractive but tasty fruit.

The Ugli fruit may elicit negative reactions from the children that hopefully will be overcome when they try the fruit and like it. Their prejudices may take the form of saying, "I won't eat that, it's funny looking" or, "I only eat apples. I don't like bumpy fruit."

Rejecting the Ugli fruit because of its appearance, or an association in the child's mind with another fruit, is prejudice because they are pre-judging the fruit without giving themselves a chance to taste it. If they taste it and like it, they will discover that their initial prejudiced reaction could have prevented them from having a positive experience.

Even if they don't like the Ugli fruit, they have still benefited from trying something new: their knowledge of the world has been expanded, and they have learned something more about what they do and do not like. Conduct the activity in this spirit.

Session Plan

Arrival

Play the song "All God's Critters" as the children arrive. It is a lively song for dancing and singing along.

Opening   10 minutes

Gather the group in a circle and light the candle or chalice. Say something like, "At our first session, we talked about racial justice and racism. These were words some of you had never heard. So far we have been doing things to help us understand racial justice, which is about being kind and fair to all people.

"We talked in the last few weeks about the beauty of all the kinds of people in the world, and all the different kinds of families. We can see on the map that our country is composed of people from different parts of the world. We know that there are many different languages and foods. We know that there are many different ways of dressing and playing, and many different ways of seeing the world. We call this diversity, and we cherish our nation's diversity."

If your congregation has little or no racial diversity, you may want to say something like, "Yet, when we look around us, in our own town, we find that most of our neighbors are the same as we are. Many of our schools and churches have the same people as our neighborhood. When we look around us, we find very few African Americans, Asian Americans, Latin Americans, or Native Americans (or Canadians) in our neighborhoods, churches, and schools. So we don't have many chances to experience the diversity of our world.

"To understand why we are separated from some of the wonderful diversity of people, we have to understand another hard word, 'prejudice'. Prejudice is an invisible wall between people. Prejudice keeps African Americans, Asian Americans, Latin Americans, Native Americans, and European Americans (Canadians) apart. Prejudice is a form of racial injustice. Today we are going to learn a little more about prejudice and how it affects us all—even people like you, who may never have heard the word 'prejudice' before."

If your congregation is racially diverse, say something like, "We have a wonderful world of diversity in our church, too—a rainbow race with people who are African American, Asian American, Native American, European American, Latin American—just like our city, and our country, and our world.

"Not all churches and schools and towns have a rainbow of people. In many communities in our country, people are separated from each other by color. To understand how this happened, you need to understand a hard word, 'prejudice'. Prejudice is an invisible wall between people. Prejudice can keep African Americans, Asian Americans, Native Americans, Latina/Latinos, and European Americans apart. Prejudice is a form of racial injustice.

"Today we are going to learn a little more about prejudice and how it affects us all—even people like you, who may not have heard the word 'prejudice' before."

Focusing   10 minutes

Bring out the snack. Say something like, "Today we are beginning with a snack, Ugli fruit." Hold it up and wait for reactions. Ask questions like, "What is it? Have you ever seen one? Have you ever tasted one? What do you think it tastes like? Do you think you'll like it?" Pass one or two around and let the children feel and smell the fruit. Encourage reactions from reticent children.

Cut up the fruit. Elicit comments as the children try it. Say something like, "Do you like it? Does it taste like you thought it would? Does it remind you of another fruit? What was your favorite part of snack today? Why?"

Say something like, "Sometimes we don't think we are going to like something different—a new food, or game, or people who are different from ourselves. But when we taste the food, or play the game, or meet and live with the people, we are glad that we did. We grow when we try new things."

"When you first saw the outside—the skin—of the fruit, you may have thought, 'Ugh—I'm not going to eat that!' That was prejudice—you made up your mind about a new experience without even giving it a chance. If you refused to eat the fruit, you'd only miss out on a piece of fruit. The fruit doesn't have any feelings; it doesn't care. But when someone looks at a person and says, 'I don't like the color of his skin,' or, 'What funny hair she has!' and refuses to get to know them or play with them, that's prejudice, too. When a person develops a prejudice against another person, feelings are hurt, and everyone loses."

Exploring   15 minutes

Reintroduce the word "prejudice" by writing the first part of the word on a card or newsprint. Say something like, "Today we have been talking about the word 'prejudice'. It's a long word, so let's break it into parts so we can understand it better. 'Pre' means before, and 'judge' means to give an opinion about something. Add 'pre' to what you think, and you are saying what you think about someone or something before you even know that someone or something.

Prejudice means to be unfair to someone before you even know that person. Did anyone pre-judge the fruit? Did you think you wouldn't like it before you even tried it?

"Have you ever had an experience where someone prejudged you? That is, when someone put you down or wouldn't let you do something just because you were a girl or a boy, or too young or too small? Have you ever seen someone being unfair to someone else when they didn't even know them?"

If it is helpful, use an example from your own experience. Use this example if you don't have another one: "I know someone who started to wear glasses in the first grade. Do you know anyone who started to wear glasses then? Well, she was the only person in her class wearing glasses, and that made her different. What do you think happened to her? First of all, she could see the teacher and the blackboard, and that was good. But some of the other first-graders thought she looked funny, so they called her names and wouldn't become her friend."

Elicit responses about this instance of prejudice to help the children understand the concept. Expand the discussion to include instances of racial prejudice. Use examples from your own experience or from news articles. Help the children identify the prejudice in each example.

Take out some baseball cards. Invite the children to show any cards they have brought in. Point out that professional baseball teams are "rainbow" teams, with players of many colors—black and brown and white (point to appropriate cards).

Say something like, "But did you know that years ago, only whites were allowed to play baseball in the American and National Leagues?

That meant that you couldn't play for the New York Yankees or the Cincinnati Reds or any other Major League team unless you were white. What do you think about that?"

Invite responses.

Introduce the story *Teammates* by saying: "Today we are going to read a true story about real people. It's about racial prejudice, and about justice and fairness. Let's see what happened in the history of baseball to give us the rainbow teams we have now."

Read the story and show the illustrations. Invite reactions and discussion.

Integrating   20 minutes

Say something like, "We know that rainbow teams are the best teams. They are more fair and more fun. Now you are going to make your own rainbow teams. They can be any kind of team you want: a 'green team' of children who want to clean up the earth, or a 'wildlife team' that wants to protect endangered species. What kind of team would you like to make?" (Invite responses.) Encourage the children to think of a variety of possibilities, not just athletic teams, although these are okay, too.

"Remember, we want to make a rainbow team with people of all colors working together."

Distribute Handout 7. Draw the children's attention to the skin tone and other colors of crayons. Invite them to decide what kind of team they are making, give their team a name, and color their handouts.

You could also have the children draw their own pictures rather than color the handout.

Another option: Have each child draw and cut out at least one person. Paste these "team members" on a posterboard and either have the children agree on the name and nature of the team, or let the team represent different things to different children without forcing consensus.

Closing   5 minutes

Gather the children and light the candle or chalice. Ask them if they were surprised by the fruit during snack time. Did it taste differently than they imagined it would? If possible, give each participant a piece of fruit, and ask them how they think their families will react to it.

Reflection and Planning

Take a few minutes to reflect on these questions and discuss them with your co-leader.

1. What was good about this session? Why?
2. What was not so good? Why?
3. What can I learn from this session to strengthen future sessions?
4. What do I need to prepare for the next session?

⑨ Harmony From Many Voices

Goals for Participants

- To see the Chicago Children's Choir as an example of a rainbow community.

Background

Previous sessions have raised awareness of a world with people of many colors and cultures. Session 9 introduces a diverse group within the Unitarian Universalist family: The Chicago Children's Choir, made up of boys and girls ages 8 to 18, which represents the racial and ethnic spectrum in the Chicago area.

The late Reverend Christopher Moore, for many years a minister at First Unitarian Universalist Church in Chicago, began building a music ministry in 1956. He thought children could sing many kinds of music—Renaissance motets and baroque, as well as folk and contemporary works. Perhaps his greatest contribution was the Chicago Children's Choir, a diverse community made up of boys and girls—red, yellow, black, brown, and white; wealthy and poor; all learning to sing together, work together, play together, live together, and share together—making lasting friendships while keeping their racial and cultural identity. He built a Unitarian Universalist children's rainbow. Moore once wrote in 1975, on the 25th anniversary of his graduation from Harvard University:

"I have been deeply concerned about this country and world in which we live. My way of attempting to help change it has been working with children and youth in and through music to assist them to a deeper understanding of the whole process of building and maintaining a culture that nourishes and ministers to its people. When dozens upon dozens of youngsters across

the usual generation gaps and in ever changing groups come to take responsibility for themselves, each other, and their teams, and when that process includes the sons and daughters of classmates and others equally fortunate side by side with street kids and those of every imaginable background and circumstance, and nothing is of importance but the persons themselves and what they are about together, then I begin to feel that there may be some substance to that American dream of the open society that we have so often preferred to mouth rather than to accept to live."

The Reverend Moore died in his sleep June 26, 1987, while attending the UUA General Assembly in Little Rock, Arkansas. The Chicago Children's Choir, now independent of First Unitarian Universalist Church, holds yearly training groups in 10 public schools for up to 1,500 young people, from whom choir members are selected. The group has performed at Chicago City Hall, in hospitals, nursing homes, and schools, and on the Oprah Winfrey Show. It has sung with the Chicago Symphony Orchestra, the Lyric Opera, and the Joffrey Ballet, and has traveled in Europe, Mexico, Japan, the United States, and Canada.

For a publicity packet that includes a color poster, write or call: Chicago Children's Choir, 1720 East 54th St., Chicago, IL 60615. Phone (312) 324-8300; Fax (312) 324-8333.

The poster is particularly valuable for introducing the choir to your children.

Materials

- An assortment of cheeses and seasonal fruits
- Cassette player and *Chicago Children's*

Choir tape
- Simple worship table: cloth, flower in vase, candle or chalice
- Materials for making simple instruments (Choose one or more instruments below or plan to make other simple instruments with which you are familiar.)

Bottle xylophone: small glass bottles; water; unbreakable pitcher; metal spoon to use as a beater; food coloring, if desired

Kitchen percussion: 6' of clothesline; string; metal kitchen utensils (strainers, eggbeaters, whisks, large spoons, etc.)

Drums: coffee and/or oatmeal containers (in different sizes if possible); duct tape; yarn; colored paper; dowels or sticks

Shakers: plastic bottles, small cans with covers, or paper plates or paper bowls; rice, beans, pebbles, bells, beads, or pasta; strong tape; stapler; colored paper; paint or markers

Stringed instruments: tissue boxes or shoeboxes; large rubber bands in various widths; popsicle sticks

Percussion: wooden blocks approximately 1 1/2 by 2 1/2 by 5"; sandpaper; thumbtacks

Preparation

- Set out the materials for making instruments.

- Choose selections from the *Chicago Children's Choir* tape and cue the tape in the player.

- Prepare the fruit and cheese for the closing.

- Set up the worship table.

Session Plan

Opening   5 minutes

Greet the children and invite them to sit in a circle. Light the candle or chalice. Invite each child to make a sound to describe how they are feeling today. You go first.

Focusing   10 minutes

Tell the children that you will be reading a sound story, in which everyone is going to make sounds together. All they have to do is listen to the story and copy what you do with your hands. Read the following story.

"One day, I woke up and everything was quiet and sunny and dry, so I headed out for a walk. It wasn't long before a soft rain started rustling the leaves of the trees.
(Rub palms of hands together slowly.)
"Then the rain started to fall a bit harder. (Rub palms briskly.)
"I walked faster. And soon great big drops of rain were falling from the sky.
(Snap fingers alternately, slowly at first, then with increasing speed.)
"Up ahead I saw a little building where I could take shelter from the rain. But the skies really opened up (pat palms on thighs) and I was soaked to the bone.
"I ducked under the eave of the building and listened to the rain come down harder (pat faster) and harder (pat faster).
"Dark clouds covered all the sky; the whole world was dark and gray. Off in the distance a little light appeared. (Start to slow the rhythm.)
"The sky got just a bit brighter. (Slow rhythm more.) And the rain clouds started to blow away. (Resume snapping fingers, quickly.)
"It wasn't long before the wall of water became a series of big, fat drops. (Snap slowly.) And the drops gave way to a gentle rain. (Rub palms briskly.)
"I could see the sun coming out from the clouds. (Rub palms slowly.) And all was quiet and sunny again." (Rub palms slower and slower, until the room is quiet.)
Say something like, "Good job! We made the sound effects together. One person alone would not have been able to make the sound of rain so well."
Introduce the Chicago Children's Choir by saying, "Today we are going to meet the Chicago Children's Choir but not in person. We will meet them through a tape. This is a group of singers ages 8 to 18—a rainbow of young people from many different backgrounds. They bring differ-

ent voices to their choir, and they must work together to make music. While they are making music they learn to appreciate their differences and to cooperate with each other."

Show the poster of the Chicago Children's Choir, if you have it. Tell the children that now they are going to make musical instruments so they can play and sing along with the choir.

Exploring   25 minutes

Direct the children to the materials you have gathered and explain the choices. The following suggestions include both cooperative and individual activities. If the children have difficulty making up their minds, tell them they will have a chance to share their instruments after they are made.

Cooperative Instruments

- *Bottle xylophone*: Line the glass bottles up on a stable surface low enough for the children to reach comfortably. Have the children pour graduated amounts of water into the bottles. If desired, put a few drops of food coloring in each bottle. To play, tap the bottles gently with a metal spoon. The pitch can be adjusted by pouring out or adding water.
- *Kitchen percussion*: Tie a length of clothesline between two chairs. Tie a piece of string to a range of metal utensils and hang them from the clothesline with a snug knot. To play, strike the hanging objects gently with a stick or metal spoon.

Individual Instruments

- *Drums*: Make drumsticks by wrapping one end of a stick or dowel to form a ball. To play, strike a coffee can that has a plastic cover. To make a more simple drum, use an oatmeal cannister and tape the cover to the cannister. A more elaborate variation requires a coffee can and duct tape: Remove one or both ends and cover the edges with duct tape to prevent cut fingers. Then cover one end with a "skin" made of strips of duct tape, each overlapping slightly. This produces a richer tone than a plastic lid. Decorate the sides of any of these drums with paper, fabric, markers, or yarn.

- *Shakers*: Fill a variety of break-resistant containers with rice, beans, beads, bells, pebbles, or pasta. Seal with strong tape. If using paper plates or bowls, have the children staple them together, face-to-face, leaving an opening through which to pour the sound-making material. Insert a stick or dowel for a handle, then close the opening with staples and tape.
- *Stringed instruments*: Use empty tissue boxes, or shoeboxes with an oval hole cut in the lid. Decorate with paper or fabric. *Carefully* stretch elastic bands width-wise (length-wise may stretch the rubber bands to the breaking point) over the open part of the box. Place popsicle sticks under the bands at the sides to improve the tone.
- *Percussion*: Use precut blocks of wood that the children can hold comfortably. Have them sand the ends if they are rough. Cover three sides with a piece of sandpaper, securing it with sturdy thumbtacks. To play, rub or bang the blocks together.

Integrating   10 minutes

When the children have finished their instruments, ask each child to demonstrate the sound of his or her musicmaker. Practice making some different sounds in concert. Create groups by having the children count off by threes. Have the ones play alone for a minute, then the twos, and then the threes. Then have all the children play their instruments together.

Gather the children in a circle and say something like, "We just made some wonderful sounds with our instruments. When instruments play together, it is called an orchestra. Now we are going to listen to a tape of the Chicago Children's Choir using their different voices like instruments. This orchestra of voices is called a choir. We will listen to a few of the songs quietly, then we will listen to them again and accompany them with our new orchestra."

Briefly tell the children about the Reverend Christopher Moore and the Chicago Children's Choir. Make it clear that Moore was a Unitarian Universalist and that this choir was originally part of a UU church program.

Play a selection from the tape and have the

children listen quietly. Then play the selection again and encourage the children to play along with the music. Have the children listen for different types of voices. Ask questions like, "How is a choir like our orchestra? How is the Chicago Children's Choir like our rainbow?" Lead the children in moving with the music in a circle or freely around the room.

Collect the instruments for use in Session 11.

Closing   10 minutes

Gather the group in a semicircle in front of the worship table. Say, "Today we are going to have a communion service in celebration of the work of Christopher Moore and the Chicago Children's Choir.

"A communion service is a way of sharing food and drink to bring people together with a common purpose and to build community, just like the Chicago Children's Choir builds community with music.

"As I light this candle, let us be quiet for a few moments while we think about our rainbow, our orchestra, the Chicago Children's Choir, and Christopher Moore."

Light the candle and invite the children to say one word or sentence about what was special today. Leaders may speak first to model this sharing. Continue until all have spoken who wish to. Distribute the cheese and fruit communion. Blow out the candle.

Reflection and Planning

Take a few minutes to reflect on these questions and discuss them with your co-leader.

1. What was good about this session? Why?
2. What was not so good? Why?
3. What can I learn from this session to strengthen future sessions?
4. What do I need to prepare for the next session?

Who Belongs Here?

Goals for Participants

- To see their country as a diverse land of immigrants.
- To understand the difficulties faced by immigrants.
- To express their understandings through a diorama project.

Background

This session returns to and reinforces the theme of racial, ethnic, and cultural diversity. Through the story of Nary, a Cambodian-American boy in the book *Who Belongs Here?*, the children will be introduced to two themes: almost all of us are immigrants or descendants of immigrants, and being an immigrant in a new land is difficult, especially with the added burden of prejudice.

Who Belongs Here? is a book within a book. In addition to Nary's story, some pages include italicized text that gives information about American immigrant history.

One way to use this book is to read the story while commenting on the supplementary information in your own words. It is important to use this material, for it offers the opportunity to enrich the story with the experiences of African Americans, Native Americans, European Americans, and Latinas/Latinos. In this way, the children see how all the groups fit together and see that their own group is included.

Materials

- A copy of *Who Belongs Here?: An American Story* by Mary Burns Knight (see Required Resources)
- 9 x 12" drawing paper
- Crayons, including skin tones
- Pencils
- Markers
- Masking tape
- Transparent tape
- A cardboard box the size of a small TV
- Paper to cover box
- Two dowels, 1" in diameter, 6" longer than the cardboard box
- A variety of ethnic breads and spreads

Preparation

- Read the story *Who Belongs Here?* and prepare to share it with the children.

- After reading the description of the diorama activity in the Integrating section, prepare a cardboard box to serve as a TV screen. Make two holes on each side of the box, one near the top and one near the bottom. The holes must be big enough to accommodate the dowels, and the dowels must be long enough to protrude from each side far enough to be grasped and rotated.

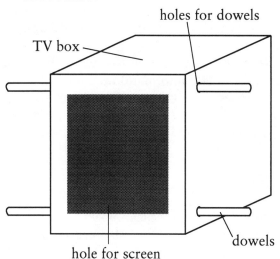

holes for dowels

TV box

dowels

hole for screen

- For a multi-cultural snack that expresses the theme of this session, arrange to have a variety of breads, such as cornbread, tortillas, matzo, pita bread, chapatis, black bread, and scones. Spreads might include peanut butter, honey, butter, or tahini.

Session Plan

Arrival

As the children arrive, engage them in covering the cardboard box with construction paper, wallpaper scraps, or used gift wrap.

Opening   5 minutes

Gather the children in a circle and light the candle or chalice. Explain that today the group will put on a show by making a diorama. A diorama is like a video on paper that will be shown on their own "TV."

Say something like, "We have been talking every week about diversity—the rainbow of people in the world and in our country. How did so many different people come to live in this country?" Invite responses and discussion, allowing the children to say what they already know and believe about our diverse population.

Focusing   15 minutes

Introduce "Who Belongs Here?" by explaining that it is a story about a boy who came all the way from Cambodia to the United States, and by pointing out Cambodia and the United States on the map.

Read the story and show the illustrations. Share some of the information about other immigrant experiences in your own words, making connections to your group, what they learned in earlier sessions, and the racial and ethnic history of your area.

Invite discussion after the story with questions such as:

- Why did Nary leave Cambodia?
- Could Nary speak English when he came to America?

- What would you do if you moved to a country where no one spoke English?
- Does anyone in your family speak other languages?
- What does Nary like about the United States?
- What doesn't he like?
- Why did some children call him names?
- Was that fair?
- What could you do if someone called you names?
- What could you do if someone called your friend names?
- How would you feel?

Ask, "Who belongs here?" Invite responses. In the course of the discussion, make the point that we all belong here.

Exploring   25 minutes

Explain that the children are going to tell Nary's story in pictures, that will be shown on their own TV. Each child should choose and episode from the book to draw and color. Help the children decide what to draw by suggesting such possibilities as:

- Nary in Cambodia.
- Nary flies to the United States.
- Nary feels sad about the war.
- Nary feels happy with his uncle and grandmother.
- Nary at the grocery store.
- Nary at school.
- Nary with his friends.
- Nary playing his drums.

Give each child a sheet of drawing paper and set out pencils, crayons, and markers. Let the children use their imaginations to respond to the story in any way that is meaningful to them.

Integrating   10 minutes

When the pictures are finished, arrange them in sequence and tape them together, bottom to top. Use masking tape on the backs and transparent tape on the fronts. You might begin the sequence with a title sheet and a credit sheet with the names of all the children. Tape a few blank sheets on each end and secure the ends to the dowels with strong tape. Roll the paper on the dowel from the end of the story toward the beginning. It should look like a scroll. Place the scroll in the box so that the title sheet is in front of the "screen."

Gather the group in front of the box. Scroll the pictures across the screen by turning one dowel, maintaining enough tension to keep the paper taut. Invite the children to narrate the parts of the story they drew.

Serve the snack of ethnic breads and spreads. Tell the children that people all over the world eat bread, but different cultures have different types of breads. Bread is another example of how we are alike, yet different.

Closing   5 minutes

Have the group stand in a circle holding hands. Light the candle or chalice. Ask, "Who belongs here?" Lead the group in raising their hands together while saying, "We all belong here!"

Reflection and Planning

Take a few minutes to reflect on these questions and discuss them with your co-leader.

1. What was good about this session? Why?
2. What was not so good? Why?
3. What can I learn from this session to strengthen future sessions?
4. What do I need to prepare for the next session?

⦙11⦙ Introducing Kwanzaa

Goals for Participants

- To learn about Kwanzaa, an African-American celebration.
- To prepare to enact a Kwanzaa celebration.

Background

During the 1960s, many African Americans adopted African traditions. They wore the dashiki and other forms of African dress. Afro (natural) hair, corn rows, and braided hair styles became popular. African art, handicrafts, literature, and culture were emphasized. The number of African American shops, bookstores, and museums increased. However, there was no national holiday to reinforce the great cultural spirit that had emerged.

In 1966 Dr. Maulana Karenga, a scholar and theorist of the Black Movement, founded Kwanzaa. It is still the only nationally celebrated, indigenous, nonreligious, nonheroic, nonpolitical African-American holiday. It is celebrated by millions of people each year.

Kwanzaa, which means "first fruits" in Swahili, is inspired by African agricultural culture and traditions.

From his studies of African societies, Dr. Karenga incorporated into Kwanzaa seven basic principles—unity, self-determination, collective work and responsibility, cooperative economics, purpose, creativity, and faith.

Traditional symbols include a seven-candle holder with red, black, and green candles, a straw mat, and corn.

Kwanzaa includes a week of festive gatherings, from December 26 to January 1, centered around food, rituals, family, and community.

Although some African Americans view Kwanzaa as a religious holiday or as an alternative to Christmas, most would agree with Bebe Moore Campbell, who writes, "It has gone through many changes and people today have streamlined the festivities to conform to their present day life styles." (*Essence* magazine, December 1986, "Celebrating Kwanzaa Now!"). One family may celebrate it on Christmas Day, another may have a Kwanzaa New Year's Eve party, and others may hold an observance in a church or club.

Kwanzaa may include storytelling, poetry recitations, music, and talent shows. However it is observed, the emphasis is on the principles and not on material things. Gifts are personal, meaningful, and usually handmade or inexpensive.

Kwanzaa is an appropriate culminating activity because it embodies many of the goals of this program. The children have experienced a sense of self worth and an appreciation of the family; they have worked cooperatively with others; they have considered likenesses and differences and learned that differences can enhance their lives; they have explored racial justice and prejudice; and they have celebrated the achievements of people who have overcome adversity.

As racial, ethnic, and cultural awareness and pride continue to grow in society, it is appropriate to learn about a distinctly African-American celebration. This session provides background and preparation for Session 12's Kwanzaa celebration, which also serves as a presentation to parents of what the children have learned in this program.

Materials

- Copies of Handout 8, "A Kwanzaa Table," for all participants
- Large sheets of posterboard
- Cassette player and tape of African music
- Brightly colored paper, such as used gift wrap or magazine pages
- Thick string, cord, or yarn
- A large, blunt plastic or metal needle for each participant
- White, clear-drying glue
- Paper labels on strings
- Pen or pencil
- Newspaper to cover table
- Popcorn popper and popcorn (optional snack)

Preparation

- Familiarize yourself with the story of Kwanzaa from the material in this session and from a resource such as *Kwanzaa: Everything You Always Wanted To Know But Didn't Know Where To Ask* by Cedric McClester (New York: Gumbs & Thomas, 1985). If possible, recruit a helper who is familiar with Kwanzaa, or someone who has lived in Africa and is familiar with the traditions on which Kwanzaa is based.

- Recruit several volunteers to help the children make necklaces.

- Cut many triangles, about two inches wide at the base and up to eleven inches long, from colorful magazine pages and brightly colored paper. (When the pictures are rolled into beads they look like abstract designs.) Read the directions for making paper bead necklaces and set out the supplies for this activity.

- Cover the work table with newspaper.

- Print the seven principles of Kwanzaa (in children's language) on posterboard:
  - Unity (*Umoja*): People working together in families and communities.
  - Self-determination (*Kujichagulia*): People speaking, acting, and deciding for themselves.
  - Collective Work and Responsibility (*Ujima*): People helping other people.
  - Cooperative Economics (*Ujamaa*): Sharing what we have.
  - Purpose (*Nia*): Making the world a better place.
  - Creativity (*Kuumba*): Making our community more beautiful and productive.
  - Faith (*Imani*): Believing in justice and a rainbow world.

- Print descriptions of the seven symbols of Kwanzaa on posterboard, along with a picture representing each.

- Read the story "Gifts of Love" (at the end of this session) and decide whether you will use it to introduce Kwanzaa.

- Color one copy of Handout 8, "A Kwanzaa Table," to show to the children.

- Set up the cassette player and tape.

- Have the instruments that the children made in Session 9 available.

- Set up popcorn popper and popcorn if you choose to provide this snack.

- Planning ahead for the next session, decide who will join the children in celebrating Kwanzaa and prepare to send invitations. Inviting parents/caregivers and other guests to join the children in their meeting space right after class and adult worship usually works well.

Session Plan

Arrival

Play the tape of African music as the children arrive. Invite the children to play their instruments to the music until all have arrived.

Opening   5 minutes

Gather the group in a circle and light the candle or chalice. Ask, "Have you ever celebrated Kwanzaa?" Let the children share what they already know about Kwanzaa.

Focusing   15 minutes

Say something like, "The music we heard this morning is from Africa, and today we are going to learn about an American holiday that comes to us from Africa. It is the African-American celebration called Kwanzaa. Have you ever heard of Kwanzaa? (Let the children say what, if any, experiences they have had with Kwanzaa.)

"Kwanzaa is a special celebration based on African farming culture. It honors the harvest. After the farmers—women, men, and children—have planted seeds that have grown into plants and produced fruits and vegetables like corn and melons and turnips, they harvest their crops and save them to eat, to sell, and to feed their farm animals during the cold winter months when most crops cannot grow.

"The Pilgrims honored their first harvest in America by having a Thanksgiving meal. Today we still celebrate Thanksgiving. When Africans were brought to America as slaves, they were not allowed to observe any of their customs or holidays. They were not allowed to use their native African languages. Many African languages and music and arts were lost to African Americans. African Americans today are very proud of their African heritage, and they created Kwanzaa to celebrate their connection to Africa, the land of their ancestors."

Show the poster of the seven principles of Kwanzaa. Explain each one, using examples from the work the children have done in this program. Invite comparisons to the seven principles of Unitarian Universalism.

Show Handout 8, "A Kwanzaa Table" explaining that the seven candles on the table represent the seven principles.

Explain that black, red, and green are the colors used in some contemporary African flags. Black symbolizes the faces of black people, red stands for blood shed by Africans and African Americans in their struggles for freedom and justice, and green represents the beauty of Africa and hope for the future of the children.

Tell the children that they will all have a picture of the Kwanzaa table to take home and color.

Exploring   10 minutes

If you choose to use a story to introduce Kwanzaa or to provide an example of how Kwanzaa might be celebrated today, read the story "Gifts of Love."

Integrating   30 minutes

Explain that the children are going to make paper bead necklaces to give away as Kwanzaa love presents next week. Show the children how to roll a paper triangle, starting with the wide end, around the needle, and glue the pointed end down to make a bead. Slide the bead along the string and continue making beads on the needle. When there are enough beads on the string, tie the ends securely.

Allow enough time for each participant to make a necklace for themselves and one to give as a gift to parents or other guests. The entire string does not have to be covered with beads—even a few beads makes a nice necklace. Label each necklace with the maker's name and leave them to dry for the next session.

Have the snack available while the children work.

Closing   5 minutes

Gather the group in a circle. Give the children copies of Handout 8 "The Kwanzaa Table," to take home to color. Introduce the seven symbols poster and help the children identify the objects on their handouts. Ask participants to bring the pictures in next week to use as decorations for the Kwanzaa celebration.

Light the candle or chalice. Hold hands and pass a peace squeeze around the circle.

Reflection and Planning

Take a few minutes to reflect on these questions and discuss them with your co-leader.

1. What was good about this session? Why?
2. What was not so good? Why?
3. What can I learn from this session to strengthen future sessions?
4. What do I need to do to prepare for the next session?

Send invitations to parents/caregivers or other guests to attend the Kwanzaa celebration after next week's class. You may want to call families and ask them to bring items for the table, such as unshelled peanuts, fruits, and vegetables.

Gifts of Love

by Norma R. Poinsett

Donna Dixon ran, kicking up dust like a baby tornado. She was mad! Coming in second in the third grade spelling bee wasn't so bad, but losing to Freda Ford, her almost-best friend, was too much. "I bet I can spell "Kwanzaa" now," Donna fussed to herself. "Kwanzaa, K-w-a-n-z-a-a, Kwanzaa," she said over and over. She glanced back at the school crowd, sure her big sister Sudie and brother Benny were poking along. She was glad Mama could hear her story without a lot of butting in.

"Bang!" the old screen door slammed. Donna klunked her book satchel on the hallway bench. "Hi, Mama," she mumbled, poking her head in the dining-room door.

"My, my!" Mama said, stopping the sewing machine. "What's wrong?"

Donna poured out the whole story. Mama knew about Kwanzaa too, because she had read the book Donna had borrowed from Mrs. Bradley, her teacher. "Mrs. Bradley wrote the word on the blackboard when she read us the story," Donna moaned. "I should have learned it."

"Only one person could be the winner, Donna," Mama said. "Everybody has to lose sometimes." Donna was beginning to feel better about Freda out-spelling her. "If I understand right," Mama said, "Kwanzaa is an African-American New Year's Party." Mama reminded Donna that the meaning of the word was most important. "'Kwanzaa' means 'first fruits', and the holiday celebrates the work we do in our family and community."

"I wish our family could have a celebration," Donna said. Already she was dreaming up a Kwanzaa party.

"Not so fast," Mama said. "That's a lot of partying. Kwanzaa starts on Christmas night and lasts for seven days."

"But it would be a *cool* long party," Donna said, hugging the Kwanzaa book in her arms. Mama started sewing again, but the whirr of the sewing machine didn't drown out Donna's voice. "And there would be gifts for seven days," Donna added. Mama cautioned her about getting her hopes up in the clouds.

When Benny and Sudie bounded in, they were surprised at Donna's happy face. "Well!" Sudie said, "What big secret lit up your world?" The dimple in Donna's chin grew deeper.

"I'm glad you feel better about the spelling bee," Benny said, noticing Donna's smile.

Shooing them out, Mama said, "Now change your clothes, eat, and tend to your chores."

As Donna fed the chickens, she pretended they were her guests at a Kwanzaa party. "Sorry your gifts are the same," Donna said. "Chopped corn and water isn't special but you seem to love them." Suddenly Donna had a bright idea! They could give farm gifts for Kwanzaa. Lots of things grew on the farm, in the woods, and on the hillsides. "Too many! Too many!" she said aloud.

"Too many whats?" Benny asked, passing Donna with a load of wood.

"Kwanzaa presents," she said.

Benny's eyes grew twice their size. "So that's what you and Mama were talking about," he said. "Give everybody a stick of stove wood," he teased, disappearing through the kitchen door. But he didn't upset Donna at all. Giving stove wood was a good idea.

By suppertime, the whole family was thinking about Kwanzaa. Donna squealed with delight when Mama said, "Since it is Donna's idea to celebrate, she should tell the Kwanzaa story at the party."

Daddy thought it was best to have only one party. "Farm folks love a big bash," he said, "but seven days would be too much." The whole family agreed to gather farm-grown things for gifts.

"That's perfect," Donna said. "My teacher, Mrs. Bradley, said Kwanzaa gifts are gifts of love."

In a few days the back porch looked like a country fair. Donna and Sudie had wrung straw for brooms, stacking them in one corner of the porch. "Old lady Lovie Battle will appreciate a good straw broom," Donna said, and Sudie agreed. Nearby, gunny sacks full of hen-nest hay bulged like stuffed dolls. This was one time Grandma Dixon would have fresh nest hay without asking. Daddy brought in a keg full of shelled seed corn. Benny and Mama had dug sassafras roots. They sparkled from a good washing, and now they were drying on the table. Pails were filled to the rim with hickory nuts, walnuts, pecans, and peanuts. And thanks to Benny, lots of holly limbs were being kept fresh in a tub of water.

On the night before Kwanzaa, the house smelled like a candy kitchen. Mama and Daddy were making pecan pralines, molasses peanut brittle, molasses bread, and popcorn. "Stand back everybody," Daddy said, pouring syrup over the big pan of popcorn.

Donna busily buttered her fingers. "I'll wrap while Sudie and Bennie make the popcorn balls," she said. Waxed paper began rattling faster and faster as the balls of popcorn were handed to Donna. Every few minutes she plunked a piece of the sugary-sweet popcorn into her mouth.

At last it was clean-up time. Mama and Daddy let the children take over. But Donna got suspicious. She spied something in Mama's apron when she darted through the kitchen. "Clean every pot and pan," Mama said as she closed the back door.

Soon Daddy looked in the back door. Smiling, he said, "I guess the kitchen is clean enough." That was all Donna needed to hear. With one long jump, she was on the back porch. Hanging on the wall was a big poster!

"The Dixon's One Night Kwanzaa,"
an African Celebration
The First One Ever Held in
Learned, Mississippi
The Kwanzaa Story,
as told by Donna Dixon
Dec. 25

Donna jumped like a jumping jack. "That's the nicest sign ever!" She wished Mrs. Bradley could see it.

"Who made it?" Sudie asked. She liked it, too.

"I did," Mama chuckled. "Just an old sheet and crayons and a lot of secret work late at night."

"But, Mama," Benny said. "That's your good sheet."

"We will have made good use of it," Daddy said, "if the party turns out right."

"I hope we use it until it falls apart," Donna added. She was too excited to wait for Christmas night. "A Kwanzaa of love," Donna beamed. This was going to be the best Christmas they had ever had. Donna made up a song in the tune of *Give Me That Old Time Religion*:

"Giving some good old Kwanzaa
    goodies,
Giving some good old Kwanzaa goodies,
Giving some good old Kwanzaa goodies,
They're Kwanzaa gifts of love!"

Soon the whole family joined in singing the song over and over. Late that night when Donna had snuggled down in bed, too keyed up to fall asleep, she kept humming the song that soon became a gentle snore.

⦙12⦙ Celebrating Kwanzaa

Goals for Participants

- To enact a Kwanzaa celebration with their guests.
- To relate what they have learned in this program to the principles of Kwanzaa.
- To display many of the projects they have made.
- To feel a sense of accomplishment and closure.

Background

It is important that parents and the larger congregation share some of the experiences the children have had with this program. This culminating session provides an opportunity to share both the Kwanzaa celebration and the children's work from previous sessions.

The form that this sharing takes can vary considerably: Feel free to adapt the following guidelines to fit your situation.

We suggest that the presentation take place immediately after the adult worship service so that parents and other guests can join the children in their meeting room or other appropriate space.

We also suggest that the program contain these elements: a display of the children's work, such as the people rainbow, footprint banner, TV diorama, or world map; a Kwanzaa celebration; and a participatory activity for everyone, such as a song or responsive reading.

Materials

- Poster of the seven principles of Kwanzaa
- Poster of the seven symbols of Kwanzaa
- Straw mat
- A holder for seven candles, or seven candle holders
- Projects from previous sessions, such as the people rainbow and diorama
- Tape
- Eight candles
- Ears of corn and/or other vegetables
- Unshelled peanuts and fruit
- Popcorn popper and popcorn
- Juice
- Cups, small plates, napkins

Preparation

- Read the session plan and decide what modifications you will make for your group. Decide on the time, place, and guest list.

- Assemble the Kwanzaa table: on a straw mat, lay out ears of corn and/or other vegetables, peanuts, seven candles, and a candle to light the other seven.

- Display the children's projects in the area you will be using for the presentation. If possible, include the books you have used in this program.

- Prepare a simple script for the children describing the meaning of each project. For example, a child standing in front of the Declaration of the Rights of the Child might say, "We learned about the UN Declaration of the Rights of the Child, and we believe that every child has the same rights."

  Another child might stand in front of the world map and say, "We learned that our families come from all over the world." In front of the footprint banner, one might say,

"We learned that we are all alike, and we are all different."

- Set up the popcorn popper and materials needed to make popcorn.

- Send invitations and enlist helpers, if you have not already done so.

- Prepare a simple script for the seven principles of Kwanzaa, expressing in children's language a value relevant to them and this program. At the end of this session is a sample script adapted from the Birmingham Unitarian Church of Bloomfield Hills, Michigan. One child can read each of the seven principles.

Session Plan

Arrival   5 minutes

As the children arrive, invite them to tape up their colored-in pictures of the Kwanzaa table to decorate the room.

Opening   5 minutes

Gather participants in a circle and light the candle or chalice. Invite everyone to say what their favorite color is today (because it can change!), and why.

Focusing   15 minutes

Explain that today the group is going to celebrate Kwanzaa and share what they have learned with their guests.

Describe the celebration's short speaking parts. When the children understand the roles, encourage them to volunteer for reading lines.

Make sure that no one is pressured to speak who does not want to, and that all who wish to speak have an opportunity to do so.

Exploration   40 minutes

When the roles have been assigned, begin rehearsing for the celebration.

Have each child stand in front of the appropriate display and practice his or her lines in turn.

For the Kwanzaa ceremony, have the children stand near the Kwanzaa table and practice saying their lines and lighting the candles.

As time allows, have the children make popcorn for the celebration.

If you will be singing a song as part of the celebration, have the children practice the song with the instruments they made in Session 9.

Before guests arrive, have the children put on the necklaces they will give to their parents or other guests as Kwanzaa gifts of love.

Suggested Format for Kwanzaa Celebration and Class Presentation

Welcome and Introduction: Adult leader welcomes the guests, introduces self and other leaders, and expresses appreciation for working with the children in this program.

Presentation of Class Projects: Adult leader states briefly the goals of the program and directs the guests' attention to the children standing next to the projects that have helped them learn about diversity and justice. The children read or say their lines, highlighting the various topics and concepts they have explored.

Kwanzaa Ceremony: Adult leader briefly explains the origin and meaning of Kwanzaa. The children read or say their lines, explaining the meaning of the seven principles. Leaders or children light a candle after each principle is read. The children give their Kwanzaa gifts of love to parents or other guests.

The entire group sings a song such as "Kum Ba Ya," "We've Got the Whole World in Our Hands," or a song the children have learned from the *Rainbow People* tape.

Everyone shares a snack of popcorn, peanuts, fruit, and juice.

Reflection

Reflect on and discuss the following questions:
1. How do I feel about the entire program?
2. What have I learned?
3. Are there any resources or words of wisdom I want to leave for the people who may lead this program next time in my congregation?
4. Please photocopy the Leaders' Evaluation at the end of this program, fill it out, and send it to the Curriculum Office of the UUA. Thank you and congratulations!

Kwanzaa Candle Ceremony

Adult leader: We will say the Swahili word for each principle, then light the candle representing that principle.

- **Unity—*Umoja.*** We celebrate that we are here together. If we remember and believe in our unity with our families and our congregation, we will be strong.

- **Self-determination—*Kujichagulia.*** We are determined to make a better world by understanding people who are different from us. We know that differences make our lives more interesting and beautiful.

- **Collective works and responsibility—*Ujima.*** Together we have made banners, rainbows, and dioramas. We will remember the good we can create when we work together.

- **Cooperative economics—*Ujamaa.*** We have shared and learned from our collective efforts. These fruits symbolize our harvest of knowledge and our willingness to share.

- **Purpose—*Nia.*** Our purpose now is to create a world and a people that appreciate diversity.

- **Creativity—*Kuumba.*** We give thanks for the fruits of our creative efforts— many are shown in this room. We will use our creativity for change and growth.

- **Faith—*Imani.*** We have developed faith in each other and in ourselves. We believe that we can create a better, more just world.

13 Introducing *Cinco de Mayo*

Goals for Participants

- To learn about *Cinco de Mayo*, a Mexican celebration.
- To prepare a *Cinco de Mayo* celebration for their class or others in the congregation.

Background

For groups using this program in the second half of the year, Sessions 13 and 14 offer an appropriate spring celebration. They explore the history and tradition of *Cinco de Mayo*, one of two Mexican/Mexican-American holidays commemorating phases of Mexico's struggle for independence from European rule.

The children will hear the story of *Cinco de Mayo*, make individual *piñatas* and/or *molas*, prepare traditional food, and recreate the festive atmosphere of a modern *Cinco de Mayo* celebration for parents/caregivers and other guests.

Try to avoid the "tourist" approach to exploring this or any other ethnic celebration. This can create a "we—they" dichotomy, where the people and customs of other nations, particularly Latin and African nations, are viewed as quaint and implicitly inferior to the western, industrialized way of life. Unfortunately, many older resources available through local libraries reinforce these stereotypes.

If you are unable to obtain the resources recommended for this session locally, check with museums, universities, and other congregations for help. As you talk with the children, look for ways to relate *Cinco de Mayo* to celebrations with which the children are familiar. Let them know that Mexico is a modern, diverse, industrial North American country.

Another important part of embracing our diversity is being respectful of language. If you are not familiar with Spanish, find someone who can help with the correct pronunciation of words used in these sessions.

Materials

- Paper-bag *piñatas*: paper lunch bags; colored tissue paper; markers; paint; scraps of cloth, glue, yarn or string; and "goodies" (small toys, candies, etc.)
- Balloon *piñatas*: balloons, paper towels or blank newsprint, wheat paste, colored tissue paper, yarn or string, goodies
- *Molas*: squares of fabric or construction paper for the backing; scraps of fabric, felt, or colored paper for the design; glue; and crayons.
- A copy of one or more of the following books. The most comprehensive resource is *Kids Explore*; the others offer better historical background.

  Kids Explore America's Hispanic Heritage by the Westridge Young Writer's Workshop (Santa Fe: John Muir Publications, 1992)

  Viva México! A Story of Benito Juárez and Cinco de Mayo by Argentina Palacios (New York: Steck-Vaughn, 1993)

  Mexican Celebrations by Maria Garza-Lubeck and Ana Maria Salinas (Univ. of Texas at Austin: Latin American Culture Studies Project, Institute of Latin American Studies, 1986)

- Cassette player and mariachi music tape
- Snack: *Paletas*, to be prepared ahead, or a Mexican snack of your choice

Preparation

• Decide what form next week's celebration will take. If you plan to invite guests to your celebration, speak to the teachers, minister(s) or fellowship leader(s), the committee in charge of the social hour, and anyone else whose Sunday morning routine will be affected.

• Set up a cassette player with a tape of mariachi music. Some of the instruments used in this form resemble, but are slightly different from, instruments with which the children might be familiar. Try to find a picture of a mariachi band, and be prepared to identify these instruments.

• Gather materials for the craft project(s).

 If the children will be making papier-mâché *piñatas*, blow up the balloons and tear the paper towels into 1 1/2-inch strips.

 Prepare the wheat paste right before class.

 If they will be making *molas*, pre-cut background material and graduated sizes of simple ani-mal and plant shapes in a wide variety of bright colors. Starting with the largest, make each piece at least 3/8 inch smaller all around than the previous piece. Make a sample *mola*.

• Familiarize yourself with the story of *Cinco de Mayo*. It is important to know both the story of the original battle as well as the re-enactment and festival staged annually in Peñón, near Mexico City.

• Have the world map available and be ready to point out France, Spain, and Mexico.

• Prepare *paletas* (fruit popsicles) at least four hours before class (recipe at the end of this session), or have another snack available.

Session Plan

Opening and Focusing   10 minutes

Gather the group in a circle and light the candle or chalice. Direct the children's attention to the world map. Point out Spain, France, and Mexico and show the children that Mexico and the United States are close neighbors, sharing a border. Tell the children that Mexico is part of North America and an industrial nation, like the United States and Canada.

Say something like, "Today we will be learning about a Mexican holiday called *Cinco de Mayo*, which means fifth of May. *Cinco de Mayo* is a lot like Independence Day, or the Fourth of July, in the United States. 'Independence' is a big word; it means standing alone, or being able to make decisions and take care of yourself. It means the same thing for countries, and throughout the world people have struggled—and are still struggling—for the right to make their own decisions. How is Independence Day celebrated in the United States?"

If necessary, prompt the children with, "Have any of you ever been to a big Fourth of July parade? Have you gone to a cookout with your family and friends, and watched fireworks at night? Well, that is how *Cinco de Mayo* is celebrated. All across Mexico, but especially in a town called Peñón, people celebrate their independence day with parades, decorations, and food, centered around a big party called a *fiesta*.

"Today we will plan a *Cinco de Mayo* festival for our next meeting. We'll have a party for our class and some guests, with decorations and food."

Exploring   15 minutes

Ask the children if they have ever eaten Mexican food or played with a *piñata*. Explain that special foods and crafts are an important part of Mexican celebrations, just as they are an important part of the holidays and celebrations with which the children might be more familiar. If any of the children have a favorite Mexican food, ask the class if that is one of the things that they would like to prepare for the next session.

Tell the story of *Cinco de Mayo* from one of the resource books, or use the version at the end of this session. After you read the story, ask the children to find similarities between this celebration and holidays that are more familiar to them. Focus on common elements such as parades, special food, games, and decorations.

Integrating   25 minutes

Introduce the craft activities by saying something like, "Today we learned a little bit about the Mexican holiday *Cinco de Mayo*. We found out that decorations are an important part of this celebration, as they are for many holidays around the world. Now we are going to make some decorations for next week's *Cinco de Mayo* party." If the class will be making *piñatas*, explain that they will be making individual versions of the larger ones with which they might be familiar.

The *molas* will probably be less familiar. *Mola* is a traditional stitching craft originally practiced by the Cuña Indians of Panama. Today they are used to adorn clothing, are often incorporated into decorative wallhangings, and are sold by vendors at street fairs and festivals associated with celebrations like *Cinco de Mayo*. To make a *mola*, scraps of cloth are cut, stacked, and stitched into a stylized representation of a living thing (plant or animal). The children will make a simplified version with precut pieces of cloth or paper and glue.

Choose one or more of the following craft options. Don't make one large *piñata* for the entire group—the children may compete for the biggest handful of goodies and could be uncomfortable with the destruction of their creation.

Option 1: Paper-bag *piñatas* are good for younger children or larger classes. Have the children decorate their bag with markers, paper cutouts, and tissue-paper streamers before filling them with goodies. After the bags are decorated and filled, puff air into them and tie off with yarn or ribbon. Label them with the children's names.

Option 2: Balloon *piñatas* are a little more complex but are closer to the familiar form. Have the children lay strips of paper towels or blank newsprint in wheat paste just until damp (not too long, or they will become difficult to handle). Lay three or four layers of strips on a balloon, leaving enough space around the balloon's end to insert goodies later. Then rip pieces of colored tissue paper and lay them randomly on the wet surface. If the surface becomes too dry, spread a little paste on the balloon before placing more tissue.

Label with the children's names and set aside to dry in a safe place. After they are dry, and before the next session, puncture and remove the balloons, place a handful of goodies in each, and punch two holes in the top by the opening. Run a string through so that they can be hung up.

Option 3: To make *molas*, show the children the sample you have made and explain the steps of layering and gluing. *Molas* are usually sewn, but you can imitate the look of stitching with crayon marks placed along the edges of the cutouts. Encourage the children to be creative in their use of color. *Molas* are not meant to be realistic interpretations of living things—they are decorative and fanciful.

Label the finished *molas* with the children's names.

As the children work on their chosen project, move through the class and help any who seem to be having difficulty.

Serve the snack as the children work. If you prepared *paletas*, explain that they are a food from Mexico.

Closing   5 minutes

Gather the group in a circle with each child holding her or his *mola* (or *piñata*).

Light the candle or chalice.

Say something like, "Today we learned a little bit about how the Mexican people celebrate their struggle for freedom. We learned about *Cinco de Mayo*, and that this holiday is celebrated in a way that is familiar to most of us: with parades, decorations, and special foods.

"Next week we will have a *Cinco de Mayo* celebration in our class (after church). We will be learning a little more about Mexico as we make some food to share. The *molas* (*piñatas*) you made today are wonderful. I love seeing how different each one is and how beautiful they all are together."

Encourage the children to show the class their projects, perhaps telling why they chose to decorate their *piñata* as they did, or why they chose a particular animal or plant for their *mola*. Holding hands, draw closer to the chalice and gently blow it out together.

Reflection and Planning

Take a few minutes to reflect on these questions and discuss them with your co-leader.

1. What was good about this session? Why?
2. What was not so good? Why?
3. What can I learn from this session to strengthen future sessions?
4. What do I need to prepare for the next session?

Paletas (Fruit Popsicles)

- 2 cups puréed fruit (strawberries and peaches are sweet enough to work without much added sugar)
- 1 cup orange juice
- 1 to 2 tablespoons sugar (to taste)
- 1/2 teaspoon lime juice (to preserve the color of the pureed fruit)

Mash the fruit in a blender, food processor, or bowl. Add fruit juice, sugar, and lime juice. Pour into two ice-cube trays and place a wooden coffee stirrer or popsicle stick in each one. Freeze until solid, 4 or more hours.

The Story of *Cinco de Mayo*

The people of Mexico had to struggle for a long time to regain their independence from European rule. In fact, they had to fight the influence of two different countries, Spain and France.

In 1810, under the leadership of a Catholic priest named Father Miguel Hidalgo, they began the fight against Spanish rule. Today, September 16 is observed as Mexican Independence Day. But the struggle was not over.

In 1862, the French Emperor Napoleon III decided to send ships full of soldiers to try to take over Mexico. When the Mexican people heard that these soldiers were landing, they sent troops to stop them. On the morning of May 5, the French marched into the city of Puebla. There they were met by Mexican soldiers sent to Puebla on orders from their president, Benito Juárez.

It took five years for the French to finally leave Mexico. But the people never forgot that first battle, when the Mexican soldiers surprised the French. Each year in Peñón, a town near Mexico City that has rock formations that look like the forts in the town of Puebla, a big festival is held on *Cinco de Mayo*, which means fifth of May in Spanish. There is a re-enactment of the battle, in which both women and men participate. The men were not the only people who fought for freedom; the women, *las soldareras*, went into battle as well, tending the wounded and often fighting along with the men. The festival has a parade and a *fiesta*, with decorations, games, and booths selling food and crafts.

So now, twice a year, in the spring (*Cinco de Mayo*) and in the fall (Independence Day), the people of Mexico remember the times when their foremothers and forefathers struggled to make their country free.

⋮14⋮ Celebrating *Cinco de Mayo*

Goals for Participants

- To share a *Cinco de Mayo* celebration with their guests.
- To display many of the projects they have made.
- To feel a sense of accomplishment and closure.

Background

This session includes one or two simple Mexican dishes in a celebration of *Cinco de Mayo*.

The Mexican food with which many of us are familiar—burritos, tacos, and dips—is not representative of the range of Mexican cuisine. Complex sauces and elaborate vegetable and meat dishes are just as much a part of Mexican cooking as what is commonly known as "Tex-Mex."

Since the recipes in this session are necessarily simple, try to find an illustrated Mexican cookbook in your local library to show the children some of the variety of Mexican cuisine.

It is important that parents and the larger congregation share some of the experiences the children have had with this program. This culminating session provides an opportunity to share both the story of *Cinco de Mayo* and the children's work from previous sessions. The form that this sharing takes can vary considerably: feel free to adapt the following guidelines to fit your situation.

We suggest that the presentation take place immediately after the adult worship service so that parents and other guests can join the children in their meeting room or other appropriate space. We also suggest that the program contain these elements:

- a display of the children's work, such as the people rainbow, footprint banner, TV diorama, or the world map
- a telling of the *Cinco de Mayo* story
- a participatory activity for everyone, such as a song or responsive reading.

Materials

- *Piñatas* and *molas* from the last session
- Projects from previous sessions, such as the people rainbow and instruments
- Tape or tacks to hang decorations
- Crepe paper
- Tortilla dough
- Rolling pin
- Waxed paper
- Spatula
- Ingredients to make *refritos* (refried beans) or your own favorite Mexican recipe
- Cast-iron frying pan(s) or electric frying pan (you need two pans if you make *refritos*)
- Cassette player and mariachi music tape
- Small bags so the children can take home leftovers
- Juice
- Cups, small plates, napkins
- Illustrated Mexican cookbook (optional)

Preparation

- Read the session plan and decide what modifications you will make for your group. Finalize the time, place, and guest list.

- Food preparation goes more smoothly with helpers. This is a wonderful opportunity to involve junior and senior high school youth in the children's program.

- Display the children's projects in the area you will be using for the presentation. If possible, include the books you have used in this program.

- Prepare a simple script for the children describing the meaning of each project. For example, a child standing in front of the Declaration of the Rights of the Child might say, "We learned about the UN Declaration of the Rights of the Child, and we believe that every child has the same rights." Another child might stand in front of the world map and say, "We learned that our families come from all over the world." In front of the footprint banner, one might say, "We learned that we are all alike, and we are all different."

- Prepare a short version of the *Cinco de Mayo* story for the children to read to their guests. Emphasize the theme of the struggle for independence, the fact that women were important participants in the battle, and the ways that *Cinco de Mayo* is commemorated and celebrated today.

- Prepare your food-preparation space. If you will be using a kitchen, be sure it has a working surface low enough for the children. If you are cooking in your meeting space with electric frying pans, arrange the space appropriately.

- Read the recipes at the end of this session and decide which food(s) the children will prepare. As appropriate, make some preparations at home, such as precutting vegetables. Gather all ingredients.

- Set out the plates, napkins, and serving utensils in the classroom.

- Hang, or arrange for helpers to hang, crepe paper in the meeting space.

- Set up the tape player with a mariachi music tape. If possible, find a book with a picture of a mariachi band.

- Make sure the world map is posted in the meeting space, that tables are set up for the children's creations, and projects are displayed.

- Send invitations if you have not already done so.

Session Plan

Arrival   5 minutes

As the children arrive, ask them to find their craft project(s) from the last session. Gather in a circle and light the candle or chalice. Ask everyone to take three deep breaths, slowly releasing each one. Remind the children that today they will be hosting a *Cinco de Mayo* celebration and that there will be lots to do!

Opening and Focusing   20 minutes

Tell the children about the foods they will prepare. Say something like, "Today we will be making (whatever you have chosen). Some of you have probably eaten tacos, burritos, and salsa before. We will be making some of those things today because they are quick to prepare and make good, healthy snacks.

"But there are many other kinds of Mexican food. For example, there is a fancy way of cooking turkey called *mole* (pronounced mo-lé). The sauce uses chocolate as one ingredient of a nutty, spicy sauce. (Feel free to explain another recipe of your choice.)

"Before we start preparing the food, let's take a few minutes to practice our parts and display our creations for our guests."

Have the children display their projects. Ask if anyone would like to help tell the story of *Cinco de Mayo*. Make sure that no one is pressured to speak who does not want to, and that all who wish to speak have a chance to do so. Assign parts and have the children practice them in front of the class.

Exploring   **40 minutes**

In the food-preparation area, explain that everyone will have a chance to roll tortillas and mix dip. Follow the recipes at the end of this session. If your class consists of younger children, you may want to either buy tortillas or prepare them at home.

When the food is ready, place it in serving bowls and, if necessary, bring it to the classroom.

Integrating

Suggested Format for *Cinco de Mayo* Celebration and Class Presentation

- *Welcome and Introduction:* Adult leader welcomes the guests, introduces self and other leaders, and expresses appreciation for working with the children in this program.

- *Presentation of Class Projects:* Adult leader states briefly the goals of the program. She or he then directs the guests' attention to the children standing next to the projects that have helped them learn about diversity and justice. The children read or say their lines, highlighting the various topics and concepts they have explored.

- *The Story of Cinco de Mayo:* Adult leader or children briefly explain the origin of the *Cinco de Mayo* celebration.

- *Song or Reading:* Everyone joins in a song or responsive reading.

- *Feast:* Everyone shares a snack of Mexican food prepared by the class as the mariachi music tape plays.

Reflection

Reflect on and discuss the following questions:
1. How do I feel about the entire program?
2. What have I learned?
3. Are there any resources or words of wisdom I want to leave for the people who may lead this program next time in my congregation?

4. Please photocopy the Leaders' Evaluation at the end of this program, fill it out, and send it to the Curriculum Office of the UUA. Thank you and congratulations!

Recipes

Tortillas (makes 12 to 16 tortillas)

- 4 1/2 cups unbleached flour (can substitute 1/4 cup whole-wheat flour)
- 1/2 teaspoon salt
- 3 well-rounded tablespoons of solid vegetable shortening (DO NOT use oil!)
- 1/2 cup lukewarm water

Mix dry ingredients, add vegetable shortening, and cut with two forks until mixture is crumbly. Add water by tablespoons until mixture holds together (if you add too much water, a little bit of flour will restore the mixture to a workable consistency). Roll the mixture into 1" balls. Place between two sheets of waxed paper, press flat, and continue rolling with rolling pin into a thin sheet. Place tortilla in preheated cast-iron pan or frying pan, turning when light brown spots appear. Place on plate and cover with paper towels to keep flexible until served.

Refritos (makes about 32 2-oz. servings)

- 4 16-oz. cans pinto beans, drained and rinsed
- 1 4-oz. can tomato paste
- 1 tbsp. mild chili powder
- 2 tsp. cumin (optional)
- 4 tbsp. chopped fresh cilantro or Italian parsley
- 4 scallions, finely chopped
- 2 tbsp. cooking oil
- 1 cup grated Monterey Jack or mild cheddar cheese

Mash the beans by hand or in a food processor. Heat oil in pan. Add beans, tomato paste, and spices. If beans seem too thick, add water to make a flowing paste. Cook over low heat for 10 to 15 minutes, stirring occasionally. When finished, place in bowls and sprinkle grated cheese over the top.

Symbols of Children's Rights

 The right to affection, love, and understanding.

 The right to special care if handicapped.

 The right to protection against all forms of neglect, cruelty, and exploitation.

 The right to be among the first to receive relief in times of disaster.

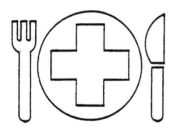 The right to adequate nutrition and medical care.

 The right to learn to be a useful member of society and to develop individual abilities.

 The right to free education and full opportunity for play and recreation.

 The right to be brought up in a spirit of peace and universal brotherhood (community).

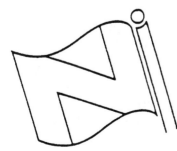 The right to a name and a nationality.

 The right to enjoy these rights, regardless of race, color, sex, religion, or national or social origin.

Declaration of the Rights of the Child

1. The right to enjoy these rights, regardless of race, color, sex, religion, or national or social origin.

   Every child has the same rights.

2. The right to learn to be a useful member of society and to develop individual abilities.

   You have the right to give your own special skills to the world.

3. The right to a name and a nationality.

   You have a right to your own name and country.

4. The right to adequate nutrition and medical care.

   You have a right to the food and medicine you need to grow up healthy and strong.

5. The right to special care if handicapped.

   You have a right to live a full life no matter what your limits are.

6. The right to affection, love, and understanding.

   You have the right to be loved.

7. The right to free education and full opportunity for play and recreation.

   You have the right to learn all you need to know, and the right to learn by playing.

8. The right to be among the first to receive relief in times of disaster.

   You have the right to get help right away when there is danger.

9. The right to protection against all forms of neglect, cruelty, and exploitation.

   You have the right to be protected from anyone who might hurt you.

10. The right to be brought up in a spirit of peace and universal brotherhood (community).

    You have the right to grow up in a world at peace, where everyone is treated as a friend.

Body Outline

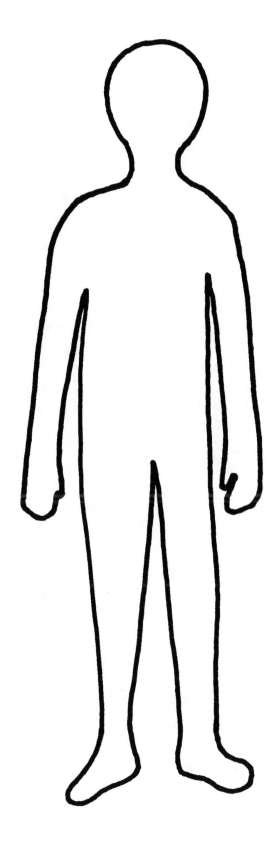

"We Come From All Over the World"

Dear Parent or Guardian:

In the first few sessions of our racial justice and diversity program, we have been getting to know each other better. This week we talked about "likenesses"; next week we'll explore "differences." To help us see each person's family differences, we invite you to talk with your child about their family's countries of origin.

We will not be doing detailed genealogies. We just want to know something of our backgrounds so that the children will appreciate the diversity in their own lives and in the lives of other members of the group. Please help your child (or children) fill out the chart below and bring it to next week's session. You can be as specific or as general as you wish. If any family members are Native Americans (or Native Canadians), please indicate, if you can, the nation and tribe (e.g., Iroquois, Tinglit) and the state or province from which they came. We will be marking all these places on a world map so that our children can see the diversity of people in our country.

Thank you!

Child's name:

Family member's name	Relationship to child	Nation/ Place of Origin

Cornucopia

Human Figures

The Rainbow Team

A Kwanzaa Table

Leader Evaluation for *Rainbow Children*

To help us assess this program, we recommend that leaders fill out photocopies of this form. Please mail your evaluations to: Curriculum Office, Religious Education Department, Unitarian Universalist Association, 25 Beacon Street, Boston, MA 02108. Thank you!

General Comments

1. How would you describe your feelings about this program?

2. How would you describe the reaction of participants to this program?

3. Were participants able to relate the material to their own lives? Were they able to share their thoughts, feelings, and experiences?

4. How did parents relate to this program?

5. How do you think participants benefited from this program?

6. What would you do differently next time?

7. What was the greatest challenge?

8. What was the highlight of the program for you?

9. Any other comments or suggestions?